IN CHARACTER

An Actor's Workbook
for Character Development

Christopher Vened

FOR KATHRYN ERVIN,

GOOD LUCK IN ALL YOUR ARTISTIC ENDEAVORS

Christoph. Vened

HEINEMANN
Portsmouth, NH

JANUARY 23, 2014

Heinemann

361 Hanover Street
Portsmouth, NH 03801–3912
www.heinemanndrama.com

Offices and agents throughout the world

Library of Congress Cataloging-in-Publication Data

Vened, Christopher.
    In character : an actor's workbook for character development /
Christopher Vened.
        p.   cm.
    Includes bibliographical references.
    ISBN 0-325-00208-8 (pbk. : alk. paper)
    1. Acting.   I. Title.
PN2061.V458   2000
792'.028—dc21

                                                    00-028145

Editor: Lisa A. Barnett
Production service: Melissa L. Inglis
Cover design: Judy Arisman
Manufacturing: Louise Richardson

Printed in the United States of America on acid-free paper
T & C Digital

For Rebecca, my wife

Contents

Foreword

This book is extremely important—in some ways it is revolutionary, because it offers the actor an integration of two apparently opposing views of character study. American acting, in both academic and studio contexts, has frequently been discussed in terms of "internal" and "external" technique. For the greater part of our century, "internal" methods have dominated the American theatre. They have tended to be adaptations of Constantin Stanislavski and, in some extreme cases, applications of psychoanalytic and psychiatric procedure. From their position of dominance, these "internal" methods have dictated the terms by which other acting systems, taught from a physical or movement perspective, have been evaluated.

The term *external* is most often employed to define a broad range of physical systems that comprise traditional conservatory training including mime, commedia dell'arte, ballet, stage combat, and period dance. But to identify a method of acting as "external" may also have pejorative connotations. Because "internal" methods frequently claim to be a means of discovering truth, they can view "external" methods, at best, as formalist impositions. At worst, "external" techniques have been seen as false or as a form of lie. This "internal/external" dichotomy in American acting training has led to a fragmented perception of the actor.

What is so compelling about Christopher Vened's book is that he invites a dialogue between the "internal" and the "external" techniques—a dialogue in which the distinctions between the two are eventually dispelled. He proposes a form of character study that is deeply personal, yet leads to a universal reference. He insists on the centrality of the individual actor, yet this very centrality is the beginning rather than the end of the actor's journey. The book urges the actor to "find yourself in the character and the character in yourself."

Because Vened speaks a dual "internal/external" language, actors drawn to the psychological approaches of Stanislavski, Michael Chekhov, and Uta Hagen, for example, will find this book as equally complementary to their work as those who are attracted to the movement-based methods of Jerzy Grotowski, Tadashi Suzuki, and Ann Bogart. It is difficult to categorize the book, however, because the discussion of character is so extraordinarily thorough and appeals to so many aspects of actor's mechanism.

If the reader is seeking antecedents, it can be argued that Vened has two progenitors or at least two very strong influences: Rudolph Laban and Henryk Tomaszewski. The precision of Laban's writing, his fusion of the scientific and the metaphysical, and his deeply felt belief that the center of all human experience is movement, has resonances in Vened's own work.

But the book is, first and foremost, a practical guide to understanding and creating character. Christopher Vened was a leading actor in Tomaszewski's Polish Mime Theatre during an extremely illustrious and distinguished period, from 1974 through 1981. Tomaszewski is a superb proponent of a particularly intense form of dramatic mime that is related to many theoretical and performance traditions including those of Laban, Russian Bio-Mechanics, Modern Dance (especially of Martha Graham, Kurt Jooss, and Mary Wigam), and the French pantomime revival of Jean Louis Barrault. From these various sources, Tomaszewski created a synthesis of methods and styles in order to arrive at his particular vision of a total movement theatre.

Vened reflects Tomaszewski's ability to draw from many different sources as a means of developing a coherent and pragmatic approach to character. He is a master teacher who offers a comprehensive system of characterization that integrates physical discipline with a complex understanding of psychology and emotional "center." His work is remarkable in that it can help the actor arrive at a high level of intensity that is associated with psychological realism, without the potential hazards of emotional dislocation.

The book can be read on different levels and can be used to serve many purposes. For both beginning and advanced actors, it offers a systematic approach for developing character. By following Vened's guide step by step, an actor will arrive at a rich and nuanced interpretation of his or her role. But the outline for character study is so complete that it can also be employed by directors and dramaturges to help them interpret character in the greater context of dramatic action. The Character Chart in Appendix A is a distillation of the entire system and is an especially invaluable reference. The book can also be viewed as a compendium of exercises related to character and could be included in classes on improvisation and theatre games. Appendix B, "Movement for the Actor," offers basic movement exercises that prepare the actor to enter into the psychophysical dialogue inherent in Vened's character system. These exercises are also useful as a general warm-up and can be performed independently.

The actors—both students and professionals—who have worked with Christopher Vened have been immeasurably enriched in their understanding of character. I am excited to have his ideas in print at last; I look forward to sharing his work with my own classes for many years to come!

MICHAEL HACKETT
Professor
Department of Theater
School of Theater, Film, and Television
University of California, Los Angeles

Acknowledgments

I should like to thank Professor Anna Krajewska and Professor Michael Hackett for reviewing my manuscript and their valuable advise and comments. Also, I thank Professor Michael Hackett for writing an excellent introduction to the book.

I would like to thank my previous students, Frances Hearn, Dana Handler, David Ellenstein, and the producer of the plays I have directed in Seattle, Robert Gallaher, for their reassuring feedback and as well for helping in an initial proofreading of the manuscript.

I wish to thank Lisa Barnett, senior editor, for her expertise on the subject of the book.

Special thanks to the actors of Wroclaw Pantomime Theater, especially to Henryk Tomaszewski, its founder and director, for endowing me with a stage experience and a practical theatrical knowledge.

Last, but the most, I would like to thank my wife, Rebecca Robertson-Szwaja for her enduring support and patronage at the time I was writing this book.

I

IDENTITY

I Am Not a Guinea Pig

When I direct, I like to think about the actor as a guinea pig on whom I experiment. I condition the actor with my assignments, direct during the process, and expect the actor to give me results. However, when I was an actor, I never thought of myself as a guinea pig and would have found it offensive if anyone else had thought of me like that. Rather, I thought of myself as an artist of self-expression and an expert on human nature, in particular the human character. I considered my work autonomous from the director's will. Of course, I fulfilled his assignment and took his direction, but it was me who knew how to execute it; it was me who invested the character with my own being; it was me who found the means of expression; and it was me who went in front of the audience and performed it. I needed the director to give me feedback, that's all. I definitely didn't need him to tell me how to do it. I knew how to do it.

There's always only one right way to do it, and that is my way. The point is to find it. Maybe it sounds to you as a lack of flexibility on my part. Well, I must assure you that's not it. If I am to be authentic, I am not able to do it any other way than my own. Acting is an act of self-identity in the fictional circumstance of the stage, and it can be accomplished only if my acting is authentic, true to myself. I may cheat my mother, my father, my lover, my child, even my audience, but I will never cheat myself.

The acting profession demands that I identify with many characters; it involves frequently changing and remaking my own psychophysical makeup. These operations can easily mess me up if I lose myself in them. Many actors do lose themselves in the character. They want so badly to identify with the character that they forget or deny their own self-identity and submit to the character unconditionally as a will-less medium or as a chameleon that wants to disguise its own presence by merging with the surroundings. This is acting by possession. The result is an audiovisual hallucination—an act strangely alienated from the actor's own nature. It looks false, and worse, it is harmful for the actor's mental and physical health. I avoid it and do not advise it. I cultivate a conscious approach to acting. I want to bring enlightenment to my audience, not confusion. My warning is: Never lose yourself in the character. My motto, which I write above the door of my rehearsal room, is "Find yourself in the character and the character in yourself." My advice is: Do everything on your own terms, according to your own measure and your own nature.

Identity

The purpose of acting is to
reveal human identity.

The root of the word *identity* comes from the Latin *idem*, meaning "same." To be identical means to be the same. The same as what? There are two meanings of identity: according to the first, it means to be the same as one's own self; according to the second, it means to be exactly the same as someone or something else. The first meaning of identity defines a person as an individual, the second as a type. Because of the concept of identity, we divide characters into two basic categories: the individual character and the character type.

How would you categorize your character?

    individual character   character type

The individual character is what makes persons different from one another; the character type is what makes them the same or similar. The individual character is unique; the character type is common or universal.

Apparently, these two character concepts exclude each other in the sense that if you are the individual character you can't be the character type and vice versa. But this may be true only in extreme cases of either personal idiosyncrasy to the point of pathological fixation or, on the other hand, total conformity. Yet the character identity of a multidimensional person (a normal person) is the combination of both the individual and the typical, or universal, character traits. It is because of this, I suppose, that the essence of human identity may be grasped, revealed, or understood as a crisscross of uniqueness and universality.

The character who has both individual and typical traits in combination is called a complex character.

5

Chameleon and Exhibitionist

> King. How do you, pretty lady?
> Oph. Well, God dild you!
> They say the owl was a baker's
> daughter. Lord, we know what
> we are, but know not what we
> may be. God be at your table!
>
> *Shakespeare*, Hamlet

Who am I on the stage: the character or myself?

The young actor often asks, "Who am I supposed to be on the stage: the character or myself?" There isn't necessarily one univocal answer to this question. For example: the character actor (called so, not quite accurately, because he specializes in portraying the character types) would answer with no hesitation, "I am supposed to be the character on the stage." The character actor is proud of being able to identify with a character as a chameleon, changing his own appearance and manner of behavior with each character to the degree that the audience is not able to recognize who is playing the part without looking at the program or credits. The character actor—or it is more accurate to call him the chameleon?—is always different in each character he portrays. "I become somebody else," he would say; "I identify with the character entirely," and "all that matters in acting is to identify with the character and to portray it all around."

Quite contrarily, the personality actor thinks that the character is only the pretext to express himself. "You are suppose to be yourself on the stage and not anybody else," he would advise you. The personality actor—or better yet, call him the exhibitionist—is always more or less the same in each part. I don't say the personality actor is "in character," because the exhibitionist does not get into the character or identify with the character on the account that it is impossi-

6

ble to be authentic when pretending to be someone else. What counts is the self-truth, the self-exposure. But what the exhibitionist really likes is the sensation of self-indulgence in showing off. Each part is yet another self-portrait of the actor. He creates this portrait by imposing on the part his own personal mannerisms, idiosyncrasies, and clichés. Sometimes it may work all right, because the personality actor specializes in portraying individual characters. Such characters are unique and idiosyncratic. And if someone is unique or idiosyncratic it's difficult or almost impossible to identify with him or her in an authentic manner. Because individual characters are unique, they are inimitable by definition. So the personality actor replaces the character's idiosyncrasies with his own personal ones.

As the chameleon likes to play with masks and disguises, the exhibitionist likes to strip his own self naked. The essential difference in their approaches is that the chameleon holds the mirror up to our nature; the exhibitionist holds the mirror up to his own nature.

It is futile to try to decide whose approach is better because both the chameleon and the exhibitionist have proved to be successful on the stage, the former in portraying character types, the latter in portraying individual characters. Yet neither the former nor the latter approach is effective in portraying the complex character, which is the combination of both the typical, or universal, and individual traits. The chameleon reduces the complex character to a grotesque caricature because he is unable to invest it with a living soul; the exhibitionist proves to be quite inadequate because he is unable to acquire characterizations other than his own clichés.

To portray the complex character, you have to be the complex actor, so it is such who is able to do both—to identify with the character and to express himself at the same time.

Exactness and Spontaneity

> To be able to portray the
> character the actor needs to
> have craft; to be able to express
> him/herself in the character the
> actor has to have talent.
> Combining these two abilities
> makes a great actor.

The actor's work proceeds in three stages: interpretation of, identification with, and self-expression in or in relation to the character. The actor interprets the character by analyzing the character's dispositions, traits, circumstances, and conduct. The actor identifies with the character by embodying the character's dispositions and by re-creating the character's speech, behavior, and action through imitation, repetition, representation, possession, empathy, and reexperiencing. In short, the actor re-creates the character's manner of being and way of conduct as exactly as possible. Yet acting is not only about re-creating the character but also about self-expression; not only about exactness but also about spontaneity; not only about the identity of the character in the play but also about the self-identity of the actor. The actor deals with two identities, one acquired and the other inherently given, merging them into one. The character from the play is an acquired identity; the actor's individual self is an inherently given—and developed—identity. Those identities may match or clash, correlate or contradict, integrate into a harmonious whole or disintegrate into an antagonistic relationship. How those two identities crisscross each other is the whole secret of acting.

Character and Incongruity

Man's character is his destiny.

Heraclitus

The audience has an interest to explore the character in drama, not only because people are curious about and intrigued by how others conduct themselves in life but also because they are uncertain how to conduct themselves in their own lives, and so they look for guidance in drama, hoping to draw a lesson for themselves.

By all means, I don't suggest that the task of the dramatist is to provide people a role model of conduct and behavior as, for example, some organized religions and ideological propaganda do, claiming that only they know the right way of conduct, the good and the same for all.

The dramatist explores the human character on the individual basis, examining individual choices of behavior and conduct, aiming to figure out the motive of human action and to foresee its consequence. This is done to show the audience how another individual copes with his or her existence and, by that, how to understand him or her better. Is it enough to satisfy the audience? Does it appease the audience's uncertainty? Does it give people guidance, or a clue, or at least a hint of how to conduct and behave themselves in their own lives?

With any luck it does, but that's not of paramount importance. Rather, it is important that the drama helps the audience realize over and over again the same fundamental truth: that we are all groping blindly in search of our own destiny, that it is a normal human condition to be uncertain about it, and that it is up to us to make our own choices in order to cope with it.

The uncertainty of destiny derives from the fact that the human being is the only creature who lacks—or almost entirely lacks—an instinctual pattern of behavior and conduct. We have to make up for it by developing a character, which, in this context, we may define as a program of behavior and conduct that is either self-made or borrowed from social convention. The self-made character is called the individual character; the character borrowed from social convention is called the character type. In both cases, the function of character is to provide structure to one's life, to organize one's behavior into habits, and to integrate one's thoughts into a personality pattern.

The problem is that the character never suits perfectly well to the person. There's almost always some degree of incongruity between one's character and one's being, causing doubts as to whether one behaves and conducts the self rightly in life and, in turn, causing discord between the self and the character, which leads to conflict, the source of drama.

II

CONFLICT

The Character's Conflict

> Rightly to be great
> Is not to stir without great
>   argument,
> But greatly to find quarrel in a
>   straw
> When honor's at the stake.

Shakespeare, Hamlet

What is the conflict of your character?

Each drama play is a particular case of the human conflict described in its course of action. The conflict is the essence of drama. The function of the drama conflict is to test or quest the character(s) to which extent she is the master of her destiny and to which extent she is merely the puppet of fate. This test or quest may be found essentially in all character conflicts.

Obstacle
With whom and what is your character in conflict?

> ASSIGNMENT: Specify persons and forces against which your character fights, struggles, or stands throughout the play.

Kind of Conflict
What kind of conflict is it?

> ASSIGNMENT: Define your character's kind of conflict.

Examples

- the domestic (family feud, clan war), ethnic, class, or generational conflict
- the conflict with society: an individual against a social authority, law, convention, prejudice, hypocrisy, superstition, or ignorance
- the conflict with God, the Devil, Death, or Nature
- the conflict with one's own destiny: rebelling against one's own life situation; crossing the barrier assigned by human destiny by trespassing the limits of what is normal, natural, moral, and comprehensible
- the existential conflict: a man fighting or refusing to fight for survival against his fellow man
- the inner conflict: between mind and body; spirit and physical nature; the base and the higher self; the rational and the irrational; the real and the false ego
- the pathological conflict with the phantoms of one's own mind
- the conflict caused by characters' differences or similarities in disposition, such as impulsiveness, egocentricity, despotism, hopelessness, an emotional coldness, lack of sexual confidence, etc.
- the conflict of sexes: between male dog and female cat; between monogamous and polygamous conduct; between heterosexual and homosexual conduct
- the conflict of revenge

Protagonist/Antagonist

Who is the protagonist and who is the antagonist in the conflict?

The main protagonist is the central character of the play. The story follows her actions and reflects her attitude predominantly. The protagonist is responsible for bringing the conflict forth, and her actions are decisive factors in how the conflict develops, and, most important, how the conflict is resolved. The antagonist is the opponent to the protagonist in a drama conflict. The antagonist opposes the protagonist's action.

The protagonist and the antagonist are distinguished by their dramatic functions:

- The protagonist acts; the antagonist counteracts.
- The protagonist strives and struggles to accomplish her objective; the antagonist resists and obstructs that objective by setting obstacles in the protagonist's way.

In some plays (for example, A *Streetcar Named Desire*), the distinction between the protagonist and the antagonist is not as clear as indicated above. The antagonist may behave as the protagonist and vice versa. Even so, the distinction between them should be possible to make.

Notice that each subplot has its protagonist and antagonist. The main characters are either the protagonist or the antagonist. The supporting characters are involved in the conflict by taking sides.

> ASSIGNMENT: Define the protagonist and the antagonist of the conflict in which your character is involved. If your character is a supporting character, determine the side on which he or she is involved: the protagonist's or the antagonist's.

The Four Climaxes

> By the complication I mean all
> that extends from the beginning
> of the action to the part which
> marks the turning point to good
> or bad fortune. The unraveling
> is that which extends from the
> beginning of the change to the
> end.
>
> *Aristotle*, Aristotle's Poetics

ASSIGNMENT: Sketch the conflict in its course of development by analyzing its main climaxes, which are (1) locking the conflict, (2) confrontation, (3) culmination, and (4) resolution.

Locking the Conflict

The conflict is locked in the first climax of the play, which is called locking the conflict.[1] The dramatic function of this climax is to begin a plot.

ASSIGNMENT 1: Point out and describe the event in which the conflict is locked.

What happens in the first main climax of the play?

- □ The conditions of the conflict (i.e., the predicament, the obstacle, or the objective leading to the conflict) are set up.
- □ The cause of conflict is introduced to the protagonist.
- □ The initial idea of the conflict becomes rooted in the protagonist's mind.

[1]*This climax is also called "the condition of the action," named so by William T. Price.*

16

   ☐ The conflict is locked. The protagonist considers entering or is tempted or decides to enter the conflict with the antagonist.

ASSIGNMENT 2: Consider the following questions.

1. What is the condition of the conflict?
2. What is the cause of the conflict?
3. How did the protagonist enter the conflict?
4. How did the protagonist lock the conflict?

Confrontation

The confrontation is the second main climax of the play. Its dramatic function is to begin the battle between the protagonist and the antagonist by bringing the conflict forth into open confrontation.

ASSIGNMENT 1: Point out and describe the event in which the conflict breaks into open confrontation.

What happens in the confrontation, the second main climax of the play?

   ☐ The protagonist brings the conflict forth into open confrontation with the antagonist, either directly or indirectly.
   ☐ The protagonist does this by committing a *deed*, which is the actual cause of conflict. That deed starts a battle that lasts until the conflict is resolved at the end of the play.
   ☐ This climax is often called "the cause of action," because the course of action for the rest of the play is caused by this climax, and because this climax sets up the quest that the action of the rest of the play must pursue.[2]

ASSIGNMENT 2: Consider the following questions.

1. What has the protagonist done or failed to do to bring the conflict forth? Describe the deed.
2. What is the quest, set as a result of the protagonist's deed, that the action of the rest of the play must pursue?

---

[2]*As described by Bernard Grebanier in* Playwriting.

17

Culmination

The culmination is a crucial climax of the play, deciding what the final outcome of the conflict might be. It functions as a turning point of the plot, inevitably determining, more or less, the direction of the action toward the resolution.

> ASSIGNMENT 1: Point out and describe the event in which the conflict culminates.

What happens in the culmination of the play?

One or a few of the following may occur in the culmination:

- Catharsis: The conflict culminates in its peak of dramatic tension, either by reaching the highest or lowest point of intensity. Metaphorically speaking, the protagonist reaches the heights of light or the depths of darkness, experiencing a moment of spiritual revelation, a mental enlightenment, or an emotional purification. It might be either a totally devastating or liberating experience, or both.
- Recognition: The protagonist recognizes the truth of a situation; comes to a realization about himself; or discovers another character's identity.
- Reversal (peripeteia): The opposite of what the protagonist planned or hoped for occurs. The protagonist's fortune or misfortune changes into its opposite.
- The Character Transformation: The character's personality begins to change; the old one begins to disintegrate, slowly disappearing, and a new one begins to form.
- The protagonist's tragic flaw or heroic valor, vice or virtue, frailty or strength is revealed.
- The protagonist either makes her winning stroke or receives her losing blow.
- The critical point of the conflict is reached. The answer is provided whether the protagonist is going to achieve the overall objective, whether he is going to win or loose the battle he has been fighting throughout the play.

18

- ☐ The protagonist may establish a new overall objective.
- ☐ The main dramatic tension may end and a new dramatic tension may be established.

ASSIGNMENT 2: Describe what the protagonist has done or failed to do to culminate the conflict.

The protagonist has committed a deed that is decisive in determining the final outcome of the conflict. In tragedy that deed is irreversible in consequence, inevitably causing the protagonist's own downfall or death. In heroic stories, that deed is not always but usually irreversible in consequence, causing either defeat or triumph for the hero. However, in comedy, or various other genres of drama such as melodrama, mystery, and so on, that deed is seldom irreversible in consequence.

Resolution

The resolution (also called denouement) is the last climax of the play, and its dramatic function is to resolve the conflict.

ASSIGNMENT 1: Point out and describe the event in which the conflict is resolved.

What happens in the resolution?

- ☐ The protagonist and the antagonist confront each other for the last time in conflict. It may be the last battle, a reconciliation, or a coming to terms with each other.
- ☐ In result, the protagonist either accomplishes her overall objective or forfeits the chance for it definitely, proving or finding out that it is beyond her reach.
- ☐ In consequence, the protagonist is either punished or rewarded for her conduct throughout the play. Indeed, it is a moment of her final downfall or glory, defeat or victory.

ASSIGNMENT 2: Consider these questions.

1. Has the protagonist achieved his overall objective? If so, how has he accomplished it? If not, why hasn't he accomplished it?
2. What is the consequence of the conflict for your character? Is he or she rewarded or punished?

Situation and Predicament

Situation may be defined as plot action frozen at any moment in its development. To use a cinematic analogy, a situation is that state of affairs visible on the screen when the moving film in the projector stops; it refers to relationships among the characters of a particular time. But a situation may also be thought of as a kind of chamber within which ideas and emotions are made to move and collide at accelerated speed.

Gregory Fitz Gerald,
Modern Satiric Stories

What is the situation of your character and how does it change throughout the play?

ASSIGNMENT: Define the situation of your character at each stage of conflict development. The stages of conflict development are marked by climaxes; in particular, by locking the conflict, confrontation, culmination, and res-olution. Each new climax alters the situation. So there should be at least five situations you can distinguish for your character:

1. the initial situation before the conflict is locked
2. the situation after the conflict is locked
3. the situation after the confrontation
4. the situation after the culmination
5. the final situation after the resolution

Predicament

> The development of a story revolves around the various attempts a protagonist makes at solving his predicament.
> —*David Howard and Edward Mabley*, The Tools of Screenwriting

What is the predicament of your character?

Predicament is a situation from which it is difficult to disentangle oneself, or it is a condition that has requirements with which it is difficult to comply. It is a state of affairs that can be dangerous, unpleasant, perplexing, confusing, embarrassing, humiliating, ridiculous, absurd, abnormal, complicated, and so on.

What and how many options does your character have to solve his or her predicament?

There may be either just one or various possible solutions to your character's predicament.

Which option has your character chosen?

The predicament necessitates or compels your character to make a difficult decision in order to solve it. Making that decision is a challenge or hazard to your character's integrity, bringing either esteem or contempt. The option your character chooses or rejects reveals the character's flaw or valor, which is often hidden or subconscious until this moment.

Has your character resolved or failed to resolve the predicament?

> ASSIGNMENT: Describe what your character has done or failed to do to solve the predicament.

Action

> Action is dramatic when it is
> caused by conflict and done in
> order to resolve it.
>
> *Krzysztof Szwaja*

What is your character doing?

ASSIGNMENT 1: Describe your character's actions in the play. List them all. Then distinguish each action by defining its beginning and end. Next describe each action separately. First describe each action in general. Do it briefly, preferably in one sentence. The point is to find an essential activity that is going on continuously throughout the entire action. You can even describe this essential activity in one word, the verb. For example: My character is . . . pursuing, seducing, hunting, dominating, resisting, escaping, destroying, complaining, persuading, quarreling, harassing, exhibiting, investigating, testing, commanding, etc.

Note: The moment the activity begins, the action begins; the moment the activity ends, the action ends.

Next, describe each action in detail, specifying what your character is doing on a moment-to-moment basis.

Elements of Action

- □ Motivation
- □ Objective
- □ Consequence

ASSIGNMENT 2: Define the motivation, objective, and consequence of your character's action.

Objective

> **Stanislavski:** When I am excited I am so wrought up I can't control myself.
>
> **Torstov:** That is because you lack creative objectives. You play tragedy in general. And any generality in art is dangerous. —*Constantin Stanislavski,* Creating a Role

What is the objective of your character?

The objective is the ultimate aim of the character's action. It is what the character wants to get, to reach, to achieve, or to become. It is for what the character strives, struggles, or fights.

There are three types of objectives: overall (also called super-objective), main, and minor. The overall objective is what your character pursues throughout the whole play. Predominately, whatever your character does in the play serves as consecutive steps in order to fulfill the overall objective. The main objectives are the objectives of the larger units of the plot, which are acts in drama and chapters in novels. A main objective ties a character's actions into a sequence, standing distinctly on its own. The minor objectives are the objectives of single actions or bits. Each action, even the smallest bit of your character, has an objective.

The objectives follow one another in succession: the smaller subordinated to the larger one, forming consecutive sequences of the plot-action structure. The minor objectives fall in line with the main objectives; the main objectives fall in line with an overall objective.

ASSIGNMENT: Define the objectives of your character. First define an overall objective, then main objectives, and then minor objectives. Knowing the overall objective in advance helps you figure out the main and minor objectives.

- □ Objectives must be clear and well-defined.
- □ Objectives must be definite, so they keep you going on the course of action through the whole play. Otherwise, you get off-track, playing drama in general, not knowing what you are aiming at and where you are going.
- □ Objectives must be true, so you believe that you can accomplish them. Otherwise, you play falsely or without conviction.
- □ Objectives must be attractive in order to excite your desires, stir your emotions, and inspire you to make a willful effort. Otherwise, you will be cold, passionless, and reluctant to act.

Motivation

> What's Hecuba to him, or he to [Hecuba,]
> That he should weep for her? What would he do,
> Had he the motive and [the cue] for passion,
> That I have? —*Shakespeare*, Hamlet

What is the motivation of the action?

Motivation is the cause of the character's action, and its function is to incite a person to perform the action. The person forms the motivation because of natural predisposition, experience in the environment, and innate character choice. In motivation, there is "the cue for passion." It stimulates, it inspires, it urges you to perform an action; it is manifested in your psychophysical system as an impulse, desire, emotion, need, or persuasive idea.

Why does your character do it?

ASSIGNMENT: Define the motivation of your character. The motivation may or may not be described in the text. Unlike the objective, the motivation often is not described in the text or is only partially described. It is not that the author conceals the motivation of the character on purpose, it is because he or she does not know what the motivation is. I am positive that whenever the writer

25

knows the motive, he or she tells us what it is. Although it is possible to write a character without the motivation, it is impossible to perform one, at least to perform it truthfully and convincingly. Therefore, in this case, the actor discovers the motivation of the character on his or her own, in one's own psychophysical system, completing the work of the author and making up for his or her shortcomings.

Note: Don't mistake the motivation with the objective. Keep in mind that the motivation is a cause and the objective is an aim of the action. The motivation is an appetite; the objective is a bait. The motivation gives you a push and the objective a pull to perform an action; the motivation stimulates you from within, the objective from outside.

Consequence

> The spirits that know
> All mortal consequences have pronounc'd me thus:
> "Fear not, Macbeth, no man that's born of woman
> Shall e'er have power upon thee."   —*Shakespeare*, Macbeth

The transliteration of the Greek word *drama* means a thing done or to do. This implies, in my interpretation, that drama is the kind of action that is irreversible in its consequence upon the doer and/or the parties involved. The premise here is that what is done cannot be undone. Certainly, this is true for tragedy but not necessarily for other types of drama such as comedy, romance, or melodrama. The difference is that in tragedy, actions are irreversible in consequence, but in other types of drama, actions are reversible in consequence. Nevertheless, in both cases, action must be consequential in order to be dramatic. However, not all of your character's actions are necessarily dramatic. Dramatic actions are those that are consecutively part of a plot, and in their effect the situation of the character changes. Nondramatic actions are those that don't relate to the plot and are only done for the reason of characterization.

What is the consequence of your character's action(s)?

> ASSIGNMENT: Describe the consequences your charac-
> ter has to bear as a result of his or her actions. Is your char-
> acter's action(s) irreversible or reversible in consequence?
> Is your character rewarded or punished in consequence of
> the action(s)? In consequence, is it a fortunate or misfor-
> tunate, good or evil action?

III

CHARACTER TRAITS

Appearance

Visualization

> ASSIGNMENT: Visualize the appearance of the character based on the description in the play. Describe his or her looks, physical characteristics, and carriage of the body.

Visualization Technique
Visualization should be done with the supervision of an instructor. Visualization technique involves bringing the actor into a hypnotic state of mind and body in order to enable him or her to visualize. In this practice, the hypnotic state is similar to that which we naturally experience when daydreaming, except that in this case, it is stimulated by the technique of relaxation. The visualizing practice looks like a spiritual séance or a psychoanalytical session when the hypnotic effect is employed. However, there is an essential difference in the approach: the actor is not hypnotized by the instructor as a will-less medium, resigned unconditionally to the instructor's command. Rather, the function of the instructor is restricted to conducting the relaxation and to posing questions during visualization, unobtrusively. The actor must be in volitional control over his or her own faculties in order to invoke a vision. In the visualizing practice, the actor is a self-governing medium, visualizing the appearance of the character by invoking its image with the power of his or her own imagination.

Relaxation Practice
The following session should be conducted by the instructor.

Take a seat on the chair in the middle of the room. Close your eyes and keep them closed until the end of the visualization. Keeping your eyes closed allows you to concentrate on your inner space of imagination, disconnecting from the distraction of the external surroundings of the rehearsal room and other actors present there.

31

Next, you are going to relax your body part by part, following these directions:

Raise your right hand up and drop it down, letting it fall inertly. Let it hang, slackened and relaxed on the side of the chair. Do the same with your left hand. Next, raise your right leg up one foot above the ground, and then drop it down on the floor, letting it fall with the weight of its own inertia. Do the same with your left leg.

Next, focus on your right leg and imagine that it is becoming very heavy. Let your right leg rest by yielding to the force of gravity. By yielding, an excess of tension is released from your muscles. To enhance the effect further, visualize in detail the bone structure of your leg and imagine the muscles disconnecting from one another.

Now, shift your focus to your left leg and repeat the relaxation practice in the same way as you did with your right leg.

Next, relax the other parts of the body, one after another, repeating the relaxation practice in the same way for each part of the body. Proceed, shifting your focus in the following order: to the right hand and arm, the left hand and arm, head and neck, nape of the neck and shoulders, chest, waist, and hips.

When you are done relaxing all the parts of the body, you are ready to visualize. If you feel any discomfort, suitably adjust your position on the chair. During the following visualization you can move, making impulsive gestures and expressions, although your body must remain in a state of inertia, yielding to the force of gravity as if you were a rag doll.

Now, visualize the appearance of the character based on the description in the play. Imagine your character being in a specific situation and circumstance of the play. Choose the situation in which an image of the character is described and appears most vivid and graphic to you.

In the beginning of the visualization, the image of the character may appear vague, as a ghost- or phantomlike figure, foggy in substance and blurry in outline. Later on, that image will gradually crystallize into a defined shape, distinctive in features and expression.

In order to stimulate the vision, manipulate the image of the character by animating its behavior and actions. While visualizing, narrate your experiences aloud, describing in detail the character's appearance and his or her behavior and carriage.

Embodiment—Imaginary Body Exercise

> *ASSIGNMENT:* When you have finished visualization, embody the image of the character that you just created in your mind. Merge in space your own real body with the imaginary body of the character: assume the position, posture, and carriage of the image and then improvise its behavior and action, following the pattern of your visualization.

Static Form Exercise

Assume the character's posture in various positions: standing, sitting, lying, and so on. Do that as if you were posing for a still picture with the intention of creating your character's self-portrait in various static positions. In order to avoid any artificiality in striking static poses, imagine yourself in the specific life situations and surroundings of the character.

The aim of this exercise is to establish the character's habitual posture in various situations.

Defining the Character's Appearance

> *ASSIGNMENT:* Describe the appearance of your character, writing it down. Describe his or her looks, physical characteristics, and carriage of the body. Point out dominating qualities and features and be specific in describing details. It will help you acquire an appropriate characterization in practice later on.

Character's Body

Compare your own physical characteristics with those of the character. In particular, compare the features and qualities that are the natural makeup of the body; these include structure and build, cast of facial features, complexion, and so on. By doing this, you will define the natural disposition of the character; and as well, you will find out whether you have a natural predisposition to embody the character.

Make a list of the differences and similarities between your own and the character's natural makeup of the body.

The Center

If a person insists on a certain program and doesn't listen to the demands of his own heart, he's going to risk a schizophrenic crack-up. Such a person has put himself off center. He has aligned himself with a program for life, and it's not the one the body is interested in at all.

Joseph Campbell,
The Power of Myth

The center focuses your whole being into one spot. It serves as the energy source of your activity. The center coordinates the movement of your body, motivating your behavior, actions, and speech.

Character Center

ASSIGNMENT: Establish the center of your character; define its location and qualities and then embody it.

Knowing the main disposition of the character helps you determine the location of the character center. In turn, embodying the character center activates the main character disposition in your own body. For example, if the main disposition of the character is gluttony, the center would be located in your belly. To embody it you might imagine your own belly as a large, soft, warm, and mushy or Jell-O-like paunch.

A. First, define the location of your character's center. For example, if the main disposition of your character is thoughtfulness, you would locate the center in your head.

35

B. Next, stimulate your center by investing it with imagined qualities. The following are some suggestions.

- For a wise man you might imagine a big, shining, and radiating center in your head.[1]
- For a narrow-minded, stupid, or fanatic man, you might imagine a small and hard center located between tensely knitted eyebrows.[2]
- For a demagogue, or a muddleheaded type of character who is deluded and misconceptualizes, you may imagine a small, tense center madly whirling around your head.
- For a shrewd man with a keenly penetrating mind, you may imagine a sharp, piercing center located a few feet outside your eyes or forehead.[3]
- For either a sly and furtive or a mistrusting and suspicious character type, you could imagine a tiny center in the corners of your eyes, shifting quickly or nervously from side to side.
- For a dishonest, crooked character type, who is devious, sneaky, and roundabout, you might imagine a snakelike center in your neck.
- A center located on the tip of your upturned chin may serve you for an arrogant, impudent, audacious, or conceited character type.
- For a fastidious, squeamish, or dainty character type who is easily disgusted, locate your center in your oversensitive, overdiscriminating nose.
- For an earthy, sensualist type of character, establish a vitality center in your nostrils and invigorate it by sniffing everything around you compulsively like a dog that recognizes and distinguishes its surroundings by the smells of odors and spices.
- For a strict and proper character type, rigorous and self-restrained in carriage, such as a typical military man or a dry,

[1] *As described by Michael Chekhov.*
[2] *Ibid.*
[3] *Ibid.*

angular spinster, establish a stiff, hard center along your spine from its base up to the neck. It will straighten your posture. You will become rigid, appearing as though you swallowed a stick or a metal rod.

- For an athletic type, young, crude, and vigorous, you would establish your center in your shoulders.

- For a hardworking man who endures strenuous effort, who is oppressed by hard labor, or who is overburdened by the weight of duty, imagine a massive center in the nape of your neck that feels as if you were carrying a heavy load on your shoulders.

- For a hustler type of character, restless, hyper, and erratic, as many speculators, solicitors, and thieves may be, you might establish a quick-shifting double center in your elbows, enabling your hands to operate in a rough, harassing manner: pushing, knocking, and shoving aside or grabbing, grasping, and snatching toward yourself.

- The center of vital energies and powers is located in the solar plexus. It is the most powerful physical center in the body. You can activate this center instrumentally by tensing the muscles of your solar plexus. You would use it whenever your character's activity is intensely alive, forceful, or impetuous.

- The center of feelings is located in the abdomen; you can imagine it as a tender spot that trembles or heaves rapidly and violently. You can awake, excite, or agitate that center instrumentally through a breathing motion. It is the center of an overly sensitive, vulnerable, moody, hypochondriac, or hysterical type of character.

- The heart is another center of feeling, through which we feel love.

- For the center of intense emotions and passions, you would imagine a burning or explosive spot in your guts, raving and raging with fury.

Note: Notice that in order to be the *character* center, a center must be established and fixed, more or less permanently, in a specific location. Also, keep in mind that the character center is established as a result of the psychological fixation and/or the habitual activity of a person.

Gravity Center

By nature, the location of your gravity center is determined by physical factors alone. These factors are the anatomical structure, build, and weight of your body and the position and movement of your body in space.

However, when employing the character center, you are affecting the gravity center of your own body by changing its location and/or investing it with psychological qualities. This is because the character center is established not only by natural factors but also by psychological factors. In fact, the character center is often established unnaturally, more or less permanently fixed in one part of the body, disregarding both the anatomical structure and the position of the body in space.

For example, while standing in an upright position, your gravity center is located in one point on the vertical line of the body, its level-height, depending on your anatomical predisposition. If you are a tall and slender person, you are naturally inclined to establish your gravity center in the upper part of the body; whereas, if you are a short and stocky person, you would be inclined to locate your gravity center in the lower part of the body. Nevertheless, you may disregard or act against the natural disposition of your body, and as a result of your character's psychological fixation, you who are tall and slender may choose to establish your gravity center in the lower part of the body, and you who are short and stocky may choose the upper part of the body. Of course it is unnatural, but so is the behavior of many characters whose dispositions you as an actor must embody. The natural gravity center is, as already mentioned, determined by physical factors only. Notice that the natural gravity center, as opposed to the character's center, is never fixed in one spot of the body permanently but changes its location whenever the body moves and alters its position in space.

ASSIGNMENT 1: Stand in an upright position and establish your gravity center in your chest on the vertical line of the body. It is a typical center for the average man you often pass on the street. Your mental attitude and emotional state are neutral. While your posture is straight, your head and neck are relaxed. Move around, initiating your movement from the center in your chest. Improvise various kinds of character types based on the center located in your chest.

For example:

1. Establish your gravity center within your chest bone and assume the carriage of a proud man. Your chest is pushed out slightly. Your expression is self-dignified.
2. In another version of the same center, assume a carriage of a vain person, exalted and lofty in expression. Your chest may curve upward, pumped up by the air of self-admiration and self-importance. Your posture is excessively extended, and you have the sensation of both tension and lightness of the body.

ASSIGNMENT 2: Establish your gravity center in your loins on the vertical line of your body. It is a natural center of energy in movement while walking, running, or playing. Relax your upper body and walk around, initiating your movement from the center. Then run in a moderate tempo. Next, run spontaneously in various tempos and directions. Improvise various kinds of character types based on the center located in your loins.

For example:

1. Assume the carriage of a drifter, wandering aimlessly. Stroll idly around at any pace that suits your fancy—wander, meander, roam, ramble.

2. Assume an overtly sensual and/or sexual carriage of the body. If sexual, you would shift your center slightly to your sexual organs.

3. Assume the carriage of a drunken person, reeling and staggering around, struggling to maintain a stable balance in the body. First, relax your whole body, loosening and slackening it. Second, move your gravity center, the loins, off the vertical line of the body in any direction—forward, backward, or sideways. Do this while keeping your feet stuck on the ground until your body is about to lose its balance. Finally, move your feet, making the necessary steps to prevent a fall. In further improvisation, you can initiate falls, exploring the gravity center when the body loses its balance.

ASSIGNMENT 3: Establish your gravity center at about the level of the knees along the vertical line of your body. Stress the weight of your body by yielding and acting with the force of gravity. Your posture is slightly loose and drooping in the upper part of the body and solid in the lower part of the body. Your feet stand strongly on the ground. Now move around, initiating your movement from the center. Improvise various kinds of character types based on the gravity center located at or below the level of your knees.

For example:

1. Assume the carriage of a laid-back person; cave in your chest loosely or sloppily and move around dragging your feet. Move slowly, lazily, or apathetically.

2. Assume an aggressive carriage of the body. Bend your upper body forward and move back and forth restlessly, stomping the ground forcefully, working yourself up into a raging fury.

3. Assume a servile carriage of the body, bending forward and lowering the whole posture.

Movement

ASSIGNMENT: Define the qualities of your character's movement, applying the categories of weight, tempo, space, and rhythm.

1. Weight: What is the weight or force of your character's movement? Is it heavy or light, strong or weak, firm or gentle, tense or relaxed, fighting or indulging, resisting or yielding?
2. Tempo: What is the tempo of your character's movement? Is it quick or slow, sudden or sustained, short or long?
3. Space: What is the shape or direction of your character's movement in space? Is it straight or wavy, direct or flexible, rigid or pliant?
4. Rhythm: What is the rhythm of your character's movement? Is it regular or irregular, free or bound, rigorous or spontaneous, steady or unsteady, fluent or erratic, flowing or staccato?

Kind of Movement

The character's kind of movement is a habitual movement of a person, and it is established as a fixed function of the anatomy. The character's kind of movement is always distinguished by singularity of function (for example, thrusting, or pressing, or gliding, or floating) and it is manifested in all types of movement exertions: expressiveness, gestures, habitual behavior, and actions. The character's kind of movement is acquired as a result of either habitual activity or psychological fixations. For example, if the character's habitual activity is fencing, the habitual kind of movement would be thrusting—a firm, direct motion, executed in straight lines, then quickly dropped or withdrawn to the initial position. However, the character doesn't have to be a fencer to be a thruster. If your character's psychological fixation is enthusiasm, optimism, or eagerness, quite likely, the habitual kind of movement would also be thrusting.

> *ASSIGNMENT:* Define your character's kind of movement and then embody it. Look over the list of kinds of movements below. Reviewing the broad range of the verbs is very useful when you are searching for either the character's overall kind of movement or the movement for a specific activity. Realize that each verb signifies a different kind of movement that should show clearly and distinctly when you embody it. While working on embodiment of the character's movement, you will find out that some kinds of movements are very easy for you to acquire because you are already familiar with them, while others are difficult to acquire because you have had little or no opportunity to practice them. Don't be intimidated by any difficulties; your anatomy is able to learn to perform any of the movements listed below, and many others that are not listed.

Examples

thrust, stab, poke, prod, pierce
punch, pound, blow, strike
slash, whip, sweep, shove
press, crush, squeeze, cut
wring, twist, squirm, convulse
stretch, extend, reach, linger
pull, drag, pluck, snatch, snap
fly, flap, flop, slap, waggle

flick, blink, brush, preen, flutter
flip, browse, toss, fling, bounce, throw
jerk, twitch, bump, rupture
shake, quiver, tremble, shiver, shudder, quake, vibrate, totter
dab, pat, tap, peck, touch, fondle, caress
glide, slide, skim, smooth, smear, smudge, rub
float, wave, waft, sway, rock
drift, wander, meander, rove, ramble
strew, scatter, spatter, spread, sprinkle, spray
stir, budge, mix, storm, burst, erupt, gush

Character Walk

ASSIGNMENT: Describe your character's walk and then embody it. Applying the four categories of movement—weight, tempo, space, and rhythm—is helpful in determining the qualities of the walk. For example, if your character has a *steady walk*, its weight or force is heavy, its tempo is slow, its form in space can be described as feet plodding flatly on the ground, its rhythm is monotonous. The more precise you are in determining and describing the qualities of your character's walk, the more successful you are going to be in embodying the walk. Look over the examples below—they may help you determine your character's walk. You will notice that some of the walk descriptions are very technical; because of this they are sometimes difficult to read smoothly. However, they read better if you practice the walk at the same time.

Examples

My character has a(n):

brisk walk: vigorous, quick, and sturdy.
belligerent walk: forceful, sudden, aggressively direct; expressing eagerness to fight; growing in intensity; marching or military rhythm.

43

swaggering walk: a broadly swaying stride, hardy in manner, expressing a bold, impudent, or arrogant attitude.

mighty walk: strong, heavy, and hard.

monumental walk: weighty, slow, deliberately formal or ceremonious in manners.

charismatic walk: strong yet gentle, firm yet light, fast yet sustained, direct yet arrested, with a longer stride than average.

steady walk: heavy, slow, and monotonous; feet plod flatly on the ground.

cautious walk: cautious yet persistent, made in firm, short steps.

lingering walk: dreamily heavy, slow, and languid.

sluggish walk: very heavy, slow, impassive, and languorous; feet shuffling on the ground reluctantly, delaying in rhythm.

flitting walk: light, quick, swift, and nimble.

bouncing walk: resilient, light, springy, and pliant.

jerky walk: rigid, abrupt, and hard; heel stomps the ground, body makes sudden turns and sharp motions in a zigzag-like pattern.

tottering walk: uncertain, hesitant, and feeble; short faltering steps; shaky knees stumbling or reeling unexpectedly.

gliding walk: elegant, smooth, and slow, with an easy, flowing, long, sliding stride.

floating walk: gentle, soft, fluently sustained sensual motion in an ebb-and-flow rhythm.

drifting walk: easy, relaxed, and flexible; carried along by the circumstances; having no particular pattern or purpose, closely related to wandering, meandering, roaming, rambling, and idling.

strutting walk: light yet tense, indulging yet self-controlled, bound in rhythm, hips slightly swaying back and forth; typical for a stylish, showy, or pretentious carriage of the body, expressing vanity, self-importance, or self-display.

Gesture

> I'm not positive that a dog wagging his tail is a gesture, but
> I'm sure that a man wagging his tail is a gesture.

The movement and form of the body become a gesture when they express a person's psychology. Otherwise they are merely a physical activity. For example, the movement of a man pounding nails into a board with a hammer is a work activity, but the movement of a man pounding violently on the table with his fist is a gesture. The movement of a person tapping the keyboard of a typewriter or computer is an activity, but the movement of a person tapping the fingertips of one hand against the fingertips of the other hand is a gesture, quite likely expressing scheming or speculating. A girl blinking her eyelids may be a natural activity for protecting the eyes from an excess of light, but it may also be a gesture expressing flirtation. The movement of a woman wringing the laundry dry is an activity, but a woman wringing her clasped hands, expressing anguish or despair, is a gesture. And so on.

> ASSIGNMENT: Find your character's habitual gestures
> through movement.

First, determine what kind(s) of movement your character expresses habitually in gestures. (Look over the list of movement types earlier in this chapter to help make the determination.)

Second, make your character's kind of movement with your hands or other parts of the body, searching for forms of gesture and investing the content of gesture with psychological (mental) associations at the same time.

While working on it, keep in mind that the three basic elements of gesture are movement, form, and content. You want to find the right correspondence among these three elements for your character. If you take movement out of gesture, it becomes a frozen gesture; if you take content out of gesture, it becomes an empty gesture; if you take form out of gesture, it is not a gesture anymore but an action.

Habitual Activity

ASSIGNMENT: Define your character's habitual activities, describing each of them in detail on a moment-to-moment basis. Then acquire them in practice, improvising, repeating, and perfecting. Make sure to mark the beginning and the end of the activity distinctly.

Temperament

The character's temperament is a more or less permanent emotional disposition of the body, manifested as a habitual emotional response, excitability, and mood. The temperament functions as an impelling emotional force of the body, stimulating vitality, expressed in tempo, rhythm, and dynamic of life. Simply, the character's temperament may be defined as the emotional state to which one is inclined to submit most often.

> ASSIGNMENT: Define the temperament of your character. The following questions will help you describe comprehensively all temperamental aspects.

1. What is the habitual emotional response or reaction of my character?
2. What kind of excitability does my character have?
3. What is the emotional state or mood to which my character is inclined to submit most often?
4. What kind of vitality does my character have?
5. What are the tempo, rhythm, and dynamic of my character's life?

Examples

My character has a(n):

fierce temperament: wild, forceful, and aggressive. He lacks self-restraint and control: he's impulsive, hasty, and violent. He is always agitated and restless, charged by both excess of vitality and intensive dark emotions. He is irritable and angry, often exploding with blind rage.
enthusiastic temperament: highly excitable and energetic. She is positive, hopeful, and optimistic.
cheerful temperament: joyful, light, bright, and vibrant. He is sympathetic, friendly, and affectionate.

jovial temperament: cordial and jolly. She is warm, hearty, and robust. She is effusive, obtrusive, and loud in manners: embracing, kissing, and back slapping indiscriminately.

hilarious temperament: extremely joyful and jocular. It is the temperament of a jester, comedian or fool. He is light-headed, free-spirited, volatile, and playful. He excites laughter, amusement, and fun.

voluptuous temperament: intensely sensual, steaming, overtly sexual and seductive.

charming temperament: sweet, lovely, and alluring. Her energies and emotions are well-balanced. She has a natural rhythm and dynamic of life: vital and sensual, spontaneous and idle, content, affectionate, and kind.

charismatic temperament: radiating with warmth, energy, and power. He is both vital and self-controlled.

serene temperament: peaceful, tranquil, and calm. She is bright and lucid. She lacks excitement and emotional agitation. She is impersonally kind and friendly.

anxious temperament: frightful, uncertain, and insecure, apprehending some undefined but anticipated danger. He is emotionally tense and agitated. He has quick, nervous reactions and is erratic, hyper, or even frantic.

vulnerable temperament: oversensitive and moody, highly impressionable. She is inclined to sentimentalism, exaltation, and sensationalism.

ascetic temperament: sober, dry, and sterile. He achieves peace of soul through purity and denial; often gloomy and easily upset.

esoteric temperament: enigmatic, obscure, and murky. It was acquired through mystical practices, inflicting supernatural spirituality and mysterious moods.

ecstatic temperament: obsessive and possessive. She finds fulfillment in the state of being overpowered with intensive euphoric emotions, usually delight and bliss. It is achieved through mediumistic spiritual practices, such as being in a trance, spellbound, intoxicated state, or in a state of rapture and frenzy. It is characteristic for dreamers, drunkards, and religious zealots.

melancholy temperament: dark, sad, and pensive. It is defined by the state of metaphysical self-absorption and a deep longing for eternity or death. There is the sensation of being suspended in time: the lingering tempo, the dreamy rhythm of life.

manic-depressive temperament: psychotic, characterized by alternating states of mania and melancholia. In one phase, he is excessively dynamic and excitable with euphoric emotions, flights of ideas, and an exaggerated mood of well-being. In the other phase, he is depressed, dispirited, dejected, and gloomy.

somber temperament: dark, gloomy, and sullen, or in turn, grim, harsh, and stern.

phlegmatic temperament: very slow, heavy, and impassive. Being emotionally cool, having a clammy humor of the body and weak organic responses, she is hard to arouse to action. This character is dull, sluggish, apathetic, or lethargic.

Dynamic

The character's movement and temperament correspond with each other, and their common denominator is a dynamic. For example, if the character has a fierce temperament it would be manifested as an explosive dynamic of movement. In turn, when one makes an explosive movement, it induces fierce qualities.

Note: The fact that the dynamic is a common denominator for both temperament and movement enables the actor to acquire instrumentally any kind of temperament through movement.

> ASSIGNMENT: Define the dynamic of your character's movement in correspondence with the temperament.

We can distinguish four primary dynamics of movement: explosive, molding, volatile, and fluid. This division corresponds with the four natural elements: fire, earth, air, and water. Your character should fit one of these four types of dynamics, though you may describe the dynamic of your character's movement in more specific terms, for example: energetic, vigorous, vibrant, restless, frantic, powerful, robust, hardy, natural, unnatural, idle, sensual, impassive, feeble, inert, stark, stern, dreamy, anemic, lethargic, and so on.

Exercises for Identifying with the Elements

1. Earth: By the movement of your hands, animate the element of earth and identify with its qualities. As a result, you will achieve a molding kind of movement.

    Give to the element of earth the qualities of clay—a firm and plastic, solid mass. Mold it by pressing, kneading, and forming. Now soften the clay with the movements of your hands. Then harden it. Crumble the clay and scatter it. Proceed to the second element—water.

2. Water: Animate the element of water by the movement of your hands and identify with its qualities. As a result you will achieve a floating movement.

    Begin by animating the movement of the water's surface. Touch the surface. Skim it gently and softly with your palms and fingers. Lead your hands along the surface, undulate the wave shapes. Gradually involve the whole body and become fluid.

    Make an ebbing and flowing rhythm, swaying from side to side in varying tempos and intensities. Make your waves torrential, raging; then quiet them again in turn. The floating kind of movement induces the sensation of calm, poise, and tranquillity. Recognize it and be affected by it. Look for a smooth transition to the element of air.

3. Air: Animate the element of air by the movement of your hands and identify with its qualities. As a result, you will achieve a flying movement.

    Imagine various volatile substances such as mist and fog, and objects such as leaves and feathers. Animate them into motion. Raise them up and let them fall down.

    Involve the whole body and identify with the movement of the element. Become volatile, light, and easily changing in form. Move up and down, in a fluid, light rhythm that can be slow or quick in tempo, depending on with which kind of volatile element you identify or interact. Proceed to the element of fire.

4. Fire: Animate the element of fire by the movement of your hands and identify with its qualities. As a result, you will achieve an explosive kind of movement.

   Begin with the small movement of your fingers, as if you were kindling a smoldering fire. Your hands move up and down in quick, explosive movements, bursting suddenly and impetuously in a series of sharp turns and zigzags.

   The image of the fire is in front of you. Your hands move as if drawing the outlines of the fire. Magnify the image of the illusory fire, involving your elbows in the zigzagging motion. Let the whole body be affected, inducing the sensation of excitement, illumination, and power.

Will

Aristotle was right: there is a
power within that molds every
form, in plants and planets, in
animals and men.

Will Durant,
The Story of Philosophy

Will is both the mental and physical disposition of the character.
Will makes decisions and commitments. Will gives commands about
what to do. Also, will is the power forcing the person to perform an
action. Through will, the character attempts to control and determine the course of his or her own life, so to speak, to master his or her
own destiny.

What does your character decide to do or what is he or she committed to?

> ASSIGNMENT: Specify your character's decisions,
> choices, and, in particular, long-term commitments and
> describe how they affect and determine your character's
> course of life, which is his or her destiny.

Kind of Will
What kind of will does your character have?

> ASSIGNMENT: Describe qualities of your character's
> will. The following questions may help you figure out the
> general concept of your character's will, the following ex-
> amples may help you get the specifics.

*Is your character's will strong or weak, decisive or hesitant, dominating or
submissive, commanding or obeying, good or ill?*

Examples

My character has a(n):

unbridled will of a young man, driven by spontaneous impulses, vigorous and wild. He's always eager to act, yet reckless, unpredictable, and unreliable in employment.

pushy will of a bully, extremely forceful, impetuous, and stubborn. She sticks to her course blindly, carrying out her enterprise despite adverse circumstances, either breaking the obstacle or her neck. She does not bend or yield to anybody; she is pushy, domineering, and oppressive.

industrious will of a hard-working person, capable of enduring long hours of steady work and of withstanding physical fatigue. He is driven by necessity, striving persistently, diligent and responsible in employment.

submissive will of a servant, dutiful and resigned, subordinated to the will of her master.

absolutely obedient will of a soldier, ready to kill or die for his country in the line of patriotic duty.

collective will of a team worker, cooperative and agreeable with a group, subordinated to its leaders, driven by wanting either to belong to something greater than herself or to participate in common benefits and profits.

authoritative will of a charismatic leader, commanding, governing, and judging. His charismatic powers lie in self-reliance in making decisions, in having faith in the high abilities of human nature, and in trusting in the goodwill of others. Though he is principled, decisive, and demanding toward his subjects, he is also magnanimous, generous, and forgiving.

despotic will of a tyrant, oppressive and abusive to her subjects. She governs with absolute power driven by personal whims, arbitrary in decision making, rigorous in application, often harsh, brutal, and cruel. Her motto is to dominate, control, and then demand unconditional subordination from her subjects.

fanatic and dogmatic will of a religious zealot, vicarious to the authority of the church, its dogma, and its concept of the God. It is fierce, mesmerizing, and possessive in application.

opportunistic will of a social climber, driven to succeed, whatever the cost; ambitious, industrious, and unscrupulous in conduct.

philanthropic will of a humanitarian person, devoted to promoting the welfare of humanity as a whole, generous and magnanimous in gesture yet, in its stereotypical caricature, inefficient in practical matters.

misanthropic will of a hermit, condemning and resenting the whole of mankind as unworthy of his moral or intellectual standards.

seductive will of a harlot, tempting men by the sexuality of her body, alluring, enticing, captivating.

self-sacrificing will of a mother, giving, caring, and protecting. She is unconditionally loyal to her child.

mediumistic will of an artist, driven by inspiration, having the power to invoke a vision and to create a form.

exacting will of a critic, discriminating, clarifying, and distinguishing; or if petty, nagging and deprecating.

superhuman will of a hero, courageous and resolute. He is driven to go and achieve deeds no one dared before; he is adventurous and risk-taking in conduct, yet steadfast and persistent. He is independent in decision making, responsible and self-challenging, striving for perfection and self-mastery.

needy will of a desperate man, intense, urgent, and compelling. He is stimulated by an instinct for self-preservation, driven to get out of trouble and to escape defeat.

despondent will of a loser, hopeless, listless, and feeble. She lost her purpose, gave up her struggle, and accepted her defeat.

aimless will of a drifter, carried along by circumstance, easily swayed, indecisive, and irresolute, yet cooperative and agreeable, often self-sacrificing.

Note: Notice that although the examples above cover a broad range of human wills, they are not strictly universal categories but specific cases. And though one of the examples may describe your character's will perfectly well, don't take that description for granted; rather, describe your character's will on your own, in your own words based on the analysis of the play and your research. Still, emulate the examples whenever one fits your character. It will speed up your work enormously.

Desire

Desire is the emotional counterpart of will. Yet desire, unlike will, arises involuntarily as an emotional urge, craving, or ache of the body to perform an action and to fulfill one's real wants and wishes. Desire functions as an emotional drive to perform an action.

ASSIGNMENT 1: Define the main desire of your character.

Examples

ambition, aspiration, emulation
vanity, self-glory, narcissism
curiosity
greed, covetousness
lust
gluttony
sloth

devotion

revenge

natural desires: hunger, thirst, sex, affection

perverted desires: exhibitionism, nymphomania, satyriasis,
   anality

morbid desires: sadism, masochism, coprophilia, necrophilia

addictive desires: for drugs, alcohol, nicotine

ASSIGNMENT 2: Define the object or objective of your character's desire.

Examples

power, fame, and glory

admiration, praise, and flattery

to find the truth

money and material goods

orgiastic pleasure

to stuff one's belly excessively

to sleep, to rest, perhaps to die

purity and chastity

spiritual fulfillment, inner completion, and beauty

self-preservation

sexual union with opposite sex and reproduction

Emotional Choice: Attraction and Repulsion

Desire, besides working as an emotional drive of an action, also functions as an emotional selector of the body. In other words, the desire makes emotional choices, it determines preference for this or that, and it discriminates what the character is going to choose or reject. Desire works in the same way as an electromagnetic force of any physical body: it either attracts toward or repulses away from the self.

What are the emotional choices of your character? To what (or whom) is your character attracted and by what (or whom) repulsed? What does your character like and dislike?

ASSIGNMENT: Define your character's emotional choices. Specify your character's attractions and repulsions.

attracted to   repulsed by

Volitional Gesture

As distinguished from the mimetic gesture which describes things, the poetical gesture which expresses emotional and spiritual inner states, or the symbolic gesture which communicates meanings through abstract signs, the volitional gesture expresses will or desire, thereby showing the character's intention and foreshadowing action.

What is your character's volitional gesture?

Examples

- Your character has the *commanding gestures of a charismatic leader*, ordering the others, yet magnanimous in intention, expressing authoritative and courageous will.
- Your character has the *threatening gestures of a tyrant*, intimidating and domineering in intention, expressing despotic will.
- Your character has the *generous gestures of an altruist*, benevolent in intention, expressing goodwill toward his or her fellow men.
- Your character has the *patronizing gestures of a rich person*, condescending in intention and supercilious in manner, giving ostentatiously to show off his or her wealth and superiority.
- Your character has the *begging gestures of a poor person*, reaching importunately his or her pitifully empty hands out for help, expressing desperate needs, hoping for charity, anticipating taking alms.
- Your character has the *praying gestures of the worshiper*, stretching his or her hands and arms in the air, expressing longing for something that cannot be grasped.[1]
- Your character has the *beckoning gestures of a harlot*, winking, nodding, and waving at men, signaling her availability and seducing them to approach and to take her body for sexual pleasure.

[1] *As described by Rudolf Laban.*

- ☐ Your character has the *resenting gestures of a misanthrope*, dismissing intruders away as if flicking off flies invading his or her space, expressing frustration and a deep desire to be left alone.
- ☐ Your character has the *ingratiating gestures of a starlet*, charming and beautiful yet self-flattering in intention, expressing vanity and need for applause.

ASSIGNMENT: Embody your character's will or desire through volitional gestures.

Begin working on volitional gesture(s) by making hand movements of taking and giving in the manner your character would do. Simply ask yourself what and how your character gives to and/or takes from others and the world, and then perform it, coming up with the imaginary hands actions and then deriving gestures from them. Practice these movements of taking and giving as long as it takes for you to come up with well-shaped gestures, distinctly articulated in form and clearly showing the character's intentions. You are working on volitional gestures this way because taking and giving are basic volitional dispositions of the character, in the sense that in the moment of exerting one's will or desire one either takes or gives.

Be aware that this approach is instrumental, so it is not natural. Naturally you are first willing or desiring, and then you are either expressing it outwardly in gestures or fulfilling it in action. But in this approach you are doing everything in reverse, in the way that first you are making gestures or performing actions instrumentally, and then, in result, you are gradually mobilizing your will power and/or awakening and stirring your desire(s).

60

Feelings

> The creation of emotion is in
> itself not always a problem. The
> creation of the right kind of
> emotion remains a continuing
> problem for the actor.
>
> *Lee Strasberg,*
> A Dream of Passion

Feelings are emotional dispositions of the body. They can be neither directly ordered by will nor guided by reason. Feelings arise on their own as an involuntary response of the body to the situation the person is in at the given moment. Through feelings the body gives signals, either pleasurable or painful, informing the person whether his or her situation is beneficial or harmful.

> ASSIGNMENT: Specify the kinds of feelings your character experiences during the play.

Look over the chart of feelings in Figure 1; it may help you select and/or specify your character's feelings. As you see in the chart, all feelings are divided into two basic categories, pleasure and pain, and they are arranged in pairs of opposition.

Cause

> ASSIGNMENT: Define the cause of your character's feelings.

1. The Situation: Describe the situation in which (or as a result of which) your character gets emotional. Point out the moment when the feelings are aroused.

The Table of Feelings

	PLEASURE			PAIN		
merriment / mirth	happiness / gladness	**JOY**	**SADNESS**	sorrow / grief	regret	
tranquility	peacefulness	**CALM**	**ANGER**	rage / fury	irritation / annoyance	
security	certainty	**CONFIDENCE**	**FEAR**	fright / panic	horror / terror	
optimism	anticipation	**HOPE**	**DESPAIR**	anguish	depression	
shock	astonishment	**SURPRISE**	**BOREDOM**	ennui	apathy	
gratification	bliss	**DELIGHT**	**DISGUST**	repulsion / revulsion	loathing / repugnance	
(romantic) romance affection	(platonic) sympathy caring tenderness	**LOVE**	**HATRED**	antipathy scorn contempt	detestation despisement	abomination abhorrence
(spiritual) reverence adoration						
gratitude / gratefulness	graciousness	**KINDNESS**	**CRUELTY**	malice	meanness	
emulation	contentment	**ADMIRATION**	**ENVY**	jealousy	indignation / resentment	
arrogance	innocence	**PRIDE**	**SHAME**	guilt	shyness	
awe	trust	**FAITH**	**ANXIETY**	suspiciousness	dread	
NEITHER PLEASURE NOR PAIN			**EITHER PLEASURE OR PAIN**			
detachment	distance	**INDIFFERENCE**	**COMPASSION**	pity	empathy	

Figure 1. *The Table of Feelings*

2. The Stimulus: What specifically stimulates your character's feelings? Define it.

Note: As distinguished from the situation that is a general cause, the stimulus is a specific cause that triggers feelings into an immediate emotional expression. The expression of feeling is an emotional re-action to specific stimulus, either external or internal.

Sentiment

Sentiments are idealized feelings produced by either mere mental projections or attachments to experiences from the past. In sentiment, feeling and idea are correlated; they permeate each other: either the idea stimulates the feeling or the feeling prompts the idea.

> *ASSIGNMENT*: Define the sentiment(s) of your character.

1. To what or whom is your character emotionally attached? It may be a memory, person, place, object, or idea.
2. What kind of sentiment does your character have? Examples: romantic, nostalgic, patriotic, religious, personal, and so on.
3. What idea stimulates your character's sentiment? Specify it.

Pathological Feelings

Feelings become pathological if they become fixed in the disposition of the person as a permanently activated emotional state. They are readily expressed without a specific stimulus and regardless of the situation. For example, one is irritated and angry all the time even though people around her are friendly and kind to her. Or one is loving and kind all the time even though people torture and crucify him. Pathological feelings are aroused without a comprehensible cause; therefore, they are nothing else but sure madness.

Thought Pattern

How does your character think?

A thought pattern is your character's habitual way of thinking. Its function is to both organize and integrate the mind into personality or ego. In other words, the thought pattern is your character's habitual way of making his or her own mind.

What does your character think?

> ASSIGNMENT: Write down your character's thoughts, selecting them from the text. Thoughts are convictions, beliefs, values, reflections, opinions, and views. They are the makeup of your character's mind.

Point of View

What is your character's point of view?

Point of view is a personal stand one takes resulting from the way one perceives, understands, and evaluates things or matters. Point of view, in its basic distinction, can be either individualistic or representative. The individual point of view is the result of the character's own authentic, personal experience and is conceived by the character's own mind; the representative point of view is adopted by the character from an already-exisiting philosophy, ideology, religion, tradition, etc.

ASSIGNMENT: Consider the following questions.

1. How does your character view matters discussed in the play?
2. What is the main characteristic of your character's point of view?

Examples

Individualistic	*Representative*
commonsensical	up-to-date
narrow-minded	provincial
idiosyncratic	cosmopolitan
logical	cosmological
absurd	fascistic
impressionistic	chauvinistic
rational	feminist
irrational	Puritan
intuitive	Catholic

Attitude

What is your character's attitude?

Attitude is the manner of expressing one's views and thoughts. The attitude shows in facial expressions and gestures and has emotional coloring. Attitude is a psychophysical personification of the point of view.

The character's attitude is fixed more or less permanently and is expressed habitually as a general disposition toward others and the world. The number of attitudes and how firmly they are established depends on the type and complexity of the character.

The simplest character type, which is called a stock character, has only one invariable attitude, expressed always in the same manner. But the complex character can have a variety of attitudes with an ability to change, develop, or drop them all together. It does not necessarily mean that the complex character has an attitude less firmly fixed than the stock character, but it means that the complex character expresses an attitude (or attitudes) in more variable manners, adjusting it according to circumstance and situation, which is unlike the stock character, who is inflexible in expression as if he or she had a mask attached to the face.

What kind of attitude does your character have?

ASSIGNMENT 1: Define your character's attitudes.

Examples

positive or negative	optimistic or pessimistic
friendly or hostile	naïve or sophisticated
rude or polite	aggressive or meek
arrogant or humble	conceited or modest
bold or timid	courageous or cowardly
cautious or reckless	prudent or extravagant

rebellious or conformist

hypocritical or candid

priggish or sensitive

dignified or indignant

venerable or scornful

decent or deceitful

kind or mean

magnanimous or petty

pretentious or frank

flattering or insulting

refined or vulgar

cynical or sincere

self-righteous or tolerant

prudish or emancipated

honorable or corrupt

respectful or disrespectful

noble or base

complaisant or spiteful

benevolent or despicable

patronizing or resentful

mischievous or proper

bitter or sweet

chaste or obscene

ASSIGNMENT 2: Embody your character's attitude.

Facial Mask Exercise

Embody your character's attitude by finding its facial expression and gestures. First, work on the facial expression and then reinforce it with gestures. For example, if your character has an optimistic attitude, simply make an optimistic face, sustaining its expression with your facial muscles as long as you can and exaggerating it as much as you can. By sustaining it you are affecting your own psychology, remaking it and acquiring the psychology of the character (in this case, an optimistic character); by exaggerating it you are speeding up an embodiment, acquiring the physicalization of the character attitude instrumentally. In addition, by exaggerating the facial expression you automatically involve your whole body, finding expressions of an attitude in gestures and postures.

As a result of this exercise, you will come up with a caricature of your character: your face is going to be distorted in a grotesque grimace (frozen like a mask), your gestures are going to be overdone, your posture will be strongly silhouetted, and you will be inclined to move in an unnatural manner, like a marionette.

These artificially exaggerated forms of expressions are suitable if you are working on the stock character (a cartoonlike character type), but if you are working on the complex character (in particular from a naturalistic play) you need to come up with subtler means of expression, adequate to your character's circumstance and situation in the play. Still, whatever character you are working on, it is rewarding to begin embodiment of the attitude by making a caricature-like expression of it. If you know how to make a caricature of your character instrumentally, you will probably be able to find subtler means of expression when it comes to performing it in the context of the play.

Notes

- If you work on the stock character, all you need to do is establish a fixed manner of expression for your character's attitude and keep in this mode through the whole performance. But if you work on the complex character, you need to express your character's attitude in the process of establishing, changing, or dropping it.
- If your character has contrary attitudes, as, for example, sweet and bitter, rude and polite, friendly and hostile, or kind and mean, and so on, you may fall into a pitfall by trying to express them at the same time. This would not work. It is impossible to express two attitudes at the same time because the human face is not able to convincingly make two facial grimaces at the same time. If you do, you become so ambiguous that no one is able to read the meaning of your expression. You can't, for example, express friendliness and hostility at the same time, but you can express them in turns, being either friendly or hostile, and switching from one to the other when or how you wish, either through an abrupt or prolonged change. The transitions between contrasting attitudes work on the principle of contradictions: one attitude generates its opposition and vice versa.
- Although it is impossible to express two attitudes at the same time, it is possible to have them at the same time, one expressed externally and the other hidden underneath—as dubious or hypocritical characters have. For example, a character can be kind on the surface and mean underneath. Not to mention such a stereotype as a holy hypocrite: having a pious face, gestures,

and words overtly expressed but vile emotions and corrupted thoughts underneath. The truth of the hypocritical character is not in what he or she expresses but in what he or she hides.

But how to express the dubious or hypocritical attitude, making sure that the audience gets not only what the character expresses externally but as well that which he or she hides? Assume the forms of expressions of the false attitude and fill it with a true content. For example, assume a face of a kind person, make all the right gestures and say all the right words, but underneath have mean thoughts and emotions. It will produce an effect of falseness. Real intentions hidden underneath by the character will pervert the pretended external mask of kindness, slightly deforming and distorting its form. It is not that you would be able to express the hidden agenda of your character, but you would be able to hint that your character is double-dealing, that there is a secret underneath, that what appears is not what it represents.

So it is good to keep in mind that whether your attitude is true or false, real or only pretend, you can express only one attitude at a time because you can't make two facial grimaces at the same time.

Kinds of Thought Patterns

What kind of thought pattern does your character have?

Examples

imaginative	demagogic
associative	factual
descriptive	narrative
poetic	scheming
psycho-analytic	meditative
intuitive	superficial
versatile	conceptual
discriminatory	abstract
dialectic	absurd
scholastic	interpretative

ASSIGNMENT: *Describe your character's thought pattern.*

Examples

☐ He has a *demagogic* thought pattern, false in reasoning. He is not concerned with finding the truth, but with proving himself to be right. Once characteristic of self-made populous leaders, now demagogism is a widespread practice among public speakers and debaters, particularly among politicians, lawyers, and preachers.

Being single-minded, he insists blandly to prove his populous ideology by reasoning falsely, distorting the truth freely, and self-contradicting whenever it is convenient to him. His followers are not logical either, so it doesn't matter. He can do without reason altogether by appealing directly to irrational popular sentiments or prejudices, with his inflammatory speeches, glowing declarations, explosive exhortations, and hyperbolic eloquence.

Point of View: contradictory, irrational, emotionally charged, ideological, propagating

Attitude: muddleheaded, condemning, scornful, aggressive, confrontational, self-righteous

☐ She has a *discriminatory* thought pattern, precise in dealing with details. She is often obsessive with those details, which makes her narrow-minded and, consequently, does not let her see the larger picture or grasp an all-embracing concept. Therefore, she functions best when instructed by others in a narrow frame of set assignments, rules, and principles.

Being practical and utilitarian, she applies her mind's effort to figuring out how things are supposed to be done. In this respect, her thought pattern is like a manual, containing exact directions and recipes.

Being morally strict and proper, she always makes a clear distinction between good and evil and voices her self-righteous judgment with ultimate certainty. She is not able to handle any ambiguity, so her moral values must be defined fundamentally. In this respect, her thought pattern is like a catechism, usually reflecting the values of the moral majority of the community in which she lives.

Being unable to deal with what is unfamiliar and unknown, she strives to define her world clearly and distinctly. Her method is to narrow the horizon of her world to a realm she can handle comprehensively, blinding herself to what is beyond, and labeling and defining everything within that realm with precise meanings. Her strive for meaning is tireless, as if her life depended on it. In this respect, her thought pattern is like a computer program with files or a dictionary with precise and neatly formed definitions and categories.

Blind adherence to principles and intolerance of any errors or imperfections, in both herself and others, makes her a severe critic. She is opinionated and exacting, often condemning. Her style of speech is dry and formal; yet sometimes her sharp tongue produces a quick, witty remark.

Point of View: principled, narrow-minded, pragmatic, utilitarian, puritanical

Attitude: attentive, responsible, dutiful, exacting, nagging, fastidious, prudish, strict, and proper

□ He has a *versatile* thought pattern, easily turning and quickly shifting between various ideas and subjects. He is always hungry for new ideas, assimilating them quickly. He has to know. He has to be informed. He is a perfect man of our information age. He doesn't like to get single-mindedly stuck on one subject for long; but instead, he prefers to deal with many at one time, thinking about them simultaneously. This is because he is more interested in relations than in the essences of ideas and things. Relations are comprehensible to him; essences are obscure (so why bother?). Comparative in method, he investigates the relations between ideas, phenomenon, and things by observing similarities and differences and by apprehending correlation and contradiction.

Being an extremely outspoken, clever, and keen talker, he takes charge of an argument, often imposing his views and not giving others a chance to speak, simply by being quicker in both mind and speech. Though logical and conclusive in his reasoning, his train of thought is sometimes hard to follow because of his erratic switching between ideas, frequent changing of subjects, and sudden digressions.

Point of View: logical, rational, digressive, informative

Attitude: self-delighting, half-mischievous, meddlesome, intellectually imposing

□ She has a *superficial* thought pattern: gliding smoothly on the surface, yet not penetrating into the depth of a given matter, whatever it might be. She avoids depth because it confuses her mind and, indeed, brings her mental troubles and sometimes, if stuck in it for too long, madness. In order to protect her sanity and, consequently, her clear views of her world, she prefers not to sink into any depth. Deep brooding is not for her. She is unable to think profoundly or at length on any subject. Her mind works the best on the surface of things and matters, apprehending quickly that which is obvious and apparent.

Absorbed with the present moment, she is disinclined to either dwell upon the past or speculate about the distant future. She is interested in what is here and now exclusively.

Her mind is shallow yet many-sided. She has interest in many subjects and various fields, knowing a little bit from each—not much, but enough to enter into conversation. She has mastered an ability to chatter about almost anything, glib, eloquent, and persuasive in tongue. She is a smooth and charming talker, neat and rounded in style, seemingly wholesome and complete in her charming remarks, yet, whether knowingly or not, she misses the substance (replacing it with charm), relying on empty slogans, clichés, and truisms.

Point of View: superficial, eclectic, truistic, obvious

Attitude: outgoing yet tactful, diplomatic, sympathetic, charming, kind, and inviting

☐ He has an *interpretative* thought pattern and the *receptive* mind of an actor. He absorbs the thoughts of others and accepts them as his own. As an actor, he memorizes the words of his part and expresses them convincingly, as if he thought those words by himself. He does so not because he is unable to produce his own thoughts and words, but because thoughts and words alone are meaningless for him unless he endows them with his spirit, investing them with subtext, feeling, and imaginary circumstances. The actor knows that what matters on the stage is the voice with which he speaks, not the voice with which the writer writes. For him, it is not important what is said but how it is said. Words alone are hollow; thoughts out of life context are dead abstractions. The essential meaning is wordless and, maybe, even thoughtless.

Point of View: adaptable to and swayable by circumstance; changing as a weathercock in the wind

Attitude: cooperative, dramatic, playful, oversolicitous, childish, infantile, self-indulgent, self-sacrificing

Space

The word *theater* is a transliteration from the Greek word *theatron* (θεαϑρον), which means "the seeing place" (also translated as the "place for watching"). Greeks also called the theater "the house of vision."

Seemingly, the Greek name for the theater already implies its essential function, which is *seeing in space*. Explaining it in obvious terms, the audience comes to the theater to see and watch the performance. The performance is an artistic vision expressed and displayed in front of the audience in time and space as if it were real. But it is not real. The performance is a mere product of an artist's imagination: fiction and illusion, conceived in the artist's mind and projected externally into the space of the theater. The theatrical space is an artistic replica of the inner space of imagination. It is not actual, it is reflective. Notice that in some respects, the inner and the theatrical spaces are the same: both are limitless in time and distance; both serve us to see, to perceive what happened in the past and to foresee what awaits us in the future.

Place

> ASSIGNMENT: Describe the place in which your character lives and acts.

1. What kind of space is it?

   Examples
   real, imaginary, fantastic, dreamlike, metaphysical, recollective, conceptual vacuum

2. How does your character relate to the place?

   Examples
   acts in harmony or in discord
   feels at home or uprooted and misplaced
   is attached or alienated or indifferent

is native or foreign; is familiar or unfamiliar
has an orientation or is lost
is expanding or contracting in space; or in psychological terms, is extroverting in or introverting from the environment

Atmosphere

> Two contrasting atmospheres cannot coexist. But individual feelings of the character, even though they may contrast with the atmosphere, can exist simultaneously with it.
> —*Michael Chekhov*, To the Actor

ASSIGNMENT: Define the atmosphere of the performance as a whole and for the particular scenes.

Some plays have only one overall atmosphere that remains the same, or almost the same, throughout the entire play. That kind of invariable atmosphere is characteristic for plays that observe the classical principle of unity in time, space, and action (as in Greek tragedy) or for various modern plays and stories in which characters are stuck in one psychological situation (as in Beckett plays and Kafka stories). If you work on this type of play, it is enough to establish one overall atmosphere for the play and keep it invariable in quality throughout the entire performance. Note that although this kind of invariable atmosphere does not change into another kind of atmosphere, it changes its own dynamic because of the dramatic development of the play.

Other types of plays and stories have more than one atmosphere. Whatever the number of atmospheres, the relation among them is that there is always one overall atmosphere that reflects the spirit of the main idea of the play, and there are other, usually a few, particular atmospheres that are either variant of or in contrast to the main atmosphere. For example, the overall atmosphere of *Hamlet* is profoundly tragic, but there are also mournful atmospheres in variance and festive and humorous ones in contrast. In this case you want to establish both the overall atmosphere and the particular atmospheres for each scene.

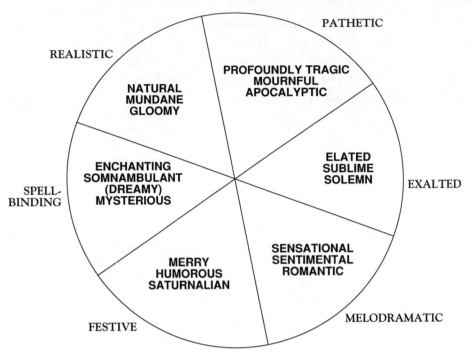

Figure 2. *Examples of Theatrical Atmospheres*

First, establish an overall atmosphere, thinking about it as the spirit of the play invoked in the real time and space of the stage. Keep in mind that if you choose the wrong atmosphere, you misrepresent the spiritual content of the play. For example, the right atmosphere is passionately romantic and you, as the result of a lack of natural passion, choose to make it merely sentimental or melodramatic. I "pray you avoid it."[1]

Second, establish the particular atmospheres for each scene, keeping in mind that each place has a specific atmosphere, and there's no such thing as a place without an atmosphere, except in the case of a conceptual vacuum—but that's not our concern now. See Figure 2 for some examples.

[1]*Shakespeare*, The Tragedy of Hamlet, Prince of Darkness (1974), 3.2.14

Object

> In the process of identification
> with the object, the actor
> undergoes objectivisation and
> the object undergoes
> subjectivization.
>
> *Henryk Tomaszewski*

Personal Object

The actor has to know how to handle all objects with which he or she is dealing during the performance, but a particular significance must be given to the personal object(s). The personal object is an object to which one is attached, and through which one expresses the self. Dramatically, the personal object of the character often functions as a catalyst of the action, initiating the character's and the audience's journey to another realm of experience, and/or prompting the character to make a commitment.

What are the objects your character is using during the performance?

> ASSIGNMENT 1: List all the objects your character is using during the performance.

> ASSIGNMENT 2: Single out your character's personal object(s).

Identification with the Object

The process of identification takes place in two stages: in the first stage, the actor identifies the object; in the second stage, the actor identifies *with* the object. Identification of the object involves establishing its qualities, condition, and function. Identification with the object involves establishing the relation between the actor and the object by the process of personification and/or objectivisation.

ASSIGNMENT: Establish the identity of your character's object and then identify with the object.

1. Qualities: Examine the object and identify its qualities. Single out the most conspicuous qualities: shape, weight, and color. Describe them. Then investigate only the material of which the object is made. Touch the surface of the object and establish tactile contact with it. Through palpable perception of your fingertips, detect the quality of the surface; in particular, determine whether it is soft or hard, smooth or harsh, hot or cold. Next animate the object in motion and invoke its imaginary sphere. Search for the expressiveness of the object, which is its image as projected to the audience.

2. Function: What is the function of the object? Describe how your character uses the object. Also define what kind of function it has, for example, utilitarian, esthetic, ceremonial, ritualistic, sacred, magical, symbolic. Then operate the object and learn how to use it.

3. Relation: Define the relation between the character and the object, and then establish your own relation with the object. Interact. Identify with the object. Keep in mind that the process of identification takes place either through personification of the object or objectivisation of the person. Finally, put the object away and visualize it from memory, establishing a mental image of the character's object in your mind. (Use the visualizing technique described in the chapter on appearance.)

Note: In particular, establish a relationship with a personal object of the character.

Relationship

> A relationship can develop and
> change even before we have met
> up with a stranger.
>
> *Uta Hagen*, Respect for Acting

Imaginary Interactions
With whom does your character interact in the play?

ASSIGNMENT 1: Identify the persons with whom your character interacts in the play.

ASSIGNMENT 2: Animate the persons into various actions in your imagination.

ASSIGNMENT 3: Interact with them through imaginary improvisation.

Kind of Relationship
There are basically two kinds of relationships: personal and social. The personal relationship is established and organized by habits, the social relationship by custom. Both of them are fixed and perfected by repetition.

ASSIGNMENT 1: Establish your character's habitual and/or customary way of relating to the other character(s) in the play. The following questions can help you explore the relationship in specific aspects and define the characters' (fixed) dispositions toward one another.

1. What kind of relationship is it?
2. What do the characters want, expect, and hope from or for one another?

3. What do they give to and/or take from one another?
4. What do they have in common that binds them together, and/or what are the differences that separate them?
5. How are they disposed toward one another?
   1. How do they get along?
   2. How do they feel about one another?
   3. How do they influence one another?
   4. What emotions do they generate in one another?
   5. What do they think about one another? What are their points of view about and attitudes toward one another?
   6. What do they do to one another? How do they treat one another? How do they behave in the presence of the others?

Interaction = Action + Reaction + Counteraction

ASSIGNMENT 2: Describe your character's interactions with another character(s) on the moment-to-moment basis. The basic structure of an interaction is action → reaction → counteraction. This structural pattern repeats itself over and over again in the course of each scene development. Follow this pattern repeatedly while setting up the blockings of the scene with your partner(s). Also point out transitions, which are the moments when the characters' dispositions toward one another change. Then interact with the other actor(s), improvising the scene.

Inner Image

> We excite our imagination only
> by what we have lost already or
> do not have yet.
>
> *Robert Musil,*
> The Man Without Qualities

Mental images are products of either perception or imagination. Perception reflects external images; imagination produces internal images. External images are immediate mental reflections of reality perceived in the present time; they are mirrorlike reflections of what we see in front of our eyes, and they are in our mind as long as we look at them. When we turn away or close our eyes, they are gone.

Internal images are quite different: they have nothing to do with reality perceived in the present time. They are either a recollection of the past or a projection to the future, as the product of pure imagination. They are not direct reflections of reality but mental pictures conceived by imagination. Their chief characteristic is that they have a life of their own, like sort of mental phantoms, independent from the reality they represent or project. Under certain conditions, the external image becomes internalized and the inner image becomes externalized. The external image becomes internalized when it is arrested in the mind longer than the time of immediate perception and is then stored in the memory. The inner image becomes externalized when it is projected into the future and then it becomes actualized.

ASSIGNMENT: Visualize the inner images of your character based on the descriptions in the play and your additional research.

In the text, your character describes or refers to these inner images whenever talking about the past or the future. These images are preset in your character's psyche as a more or less permanent visual makeup. By visualizing, you are acquiring your character's inner images, incorporating and establishing them in your own psyche. In turn, this enables you to speak your character's words as authentic expressions of your own mind because the inner images reinforce the meaning of the words with the imaginary life behind it.

Note: In some plays the inner images of the character(s) are externalized in flashbacks, visions, or invocations. These are moments of inner revelation. The mind is turned inside out and the mental or psychic phantoms appear, often—more often in classical texts than in modern ones—as ghosts, apparitions, and witches.

Inner Voice

Inner voice is a personal voice with which one talks to oneself, silently. As such, the inner voice is not meant to be shared with others. We hide our inner voice(s) from other people's ears for various intimate or obscure reasons. Yet anyone can speak one's inner voice aloud and share it with others at any time one chooses to do so. So why don't we do that? Children do it often, mad people do it all the time, and artists do it sometimes, speaking their inner voices in public. Of course everyone does it from time to time. But let me ask a rhetorical question here: Does an inner voice remain inner when one speaks it aloud? Or does it become an external voice?

Certainly, it becomes an external voice. But does it matter whether it is an internal or external voice if the only difference between them is that one is silent and the other is spoken aloud? Indeed, to a certain extent it does matter, depending on the meaning of the line and the circumstance. For example, it matters a lot whether one says such lines as "I love you" or "I hate you" aloud or in silence. The meaning is the same, but the effects may be quite different in consequence. However, if one describes what one had for breakfast this morning because one had nothing better to talk about, it doesn't matter at all whether it is silent or spoken.

There's a popular notion that extroverted people talk a lot because they are open and they tell you everything that is in their mind and heart, but introverted people don't talk much because they are hidden and they keep secrets from you, and are probably conspiring against you as well. The former are trustworthy, and the latter are untrustworthy. I don't believe such a notion at all. To accept this notion as true would mean that the external voice is sincere and the internal voice is insincere. But isn't the opposite true? Yes, it is. Certainly the inner voice is supposed to speak the truth and only the truth, but the external voice can speak not only the truth but also lies, depending on the occasion and circumstance. It would be quite a strange affair if we found one day that the inner voice was lying to us all the time. It would mean that we are not able to trust even ourselves.

ASSIGNMENT: Establish the inner voice of your character.

The inner voice is partly revealed and partly concealed in the text. Primarily the inner voice is revealed in soliloquies, which are the inner monologues of the character spoken aloud in the presence of the audience, but not in the presence of the other characters in the play. The inner voice is also revealed in any other speeches in which the character commits an act of inner exhibition or intimate confessions, such as a baring of the mind, an outpouring of the heart, a spilling of the guts, and a stripping of the soul. In other parts of the text, the inner voice is concealed as a subtext. Here, the written text seems to be an incomplete expression of the character unless there is a subtext going on in the character's mind at the same time. Observe that in this instance the character's external voice speaks the text and the internal voice speaks the subtext, simultaneously. Since in dramatic plays and scripts, as opposed to novels, the subtext is not written down, the actor must conceive it him- or herself based both on the analysis of the written text and improvisations. So we must look for the subtext behind and between the lines: behind the lines, in the ambiguity of its content; between the lines, in the unspoken meaning of the psychological pauses.

Inner Motive

Motive and Reason

> The ideal rational act would therefore be the one for
> which the motives would be practically nil and which
> would be uniquely inspired by an objective appreciation
> of the situation. The irrational or passionate act will be
> characterized by the reverse proportion.
> —*Jean-Paul Sartre*, Being and Nothingness

What is the difference between the motive and the reason for an action?

Both the motive and the reason are causes of action. The motive is
the subjective cause, while the reason is the objective cause. In other
words, the motive is a personal cause of action in the sense that it actually entices and moves a person to perform it, as distinguished from
the reason, which gives a self-justified cause to act but fails to entice
a person to actually perform it.

In fact, the reasonable cause and the motive of an action may be
incongruous with each other. Let me become personal and take you
as an example: In the moment of choosing your career you had many
reasonable causes to become a lawyer, a doctor, a businessman, and
so on, but you have chosen to become an actor. Why? What was the
cause of it? Was it reason alone? No, I don't believe that. I've never
heard any actor say so. No one becomes an actor because it is reasonable. There must be a motive that matters to you personally and
which actually moves, stimulates, or entices you to act.

> ASSIGNMENT: Distinguish and specify what is the mo-
> tive and what is the reason of your character's action.

Examples

1. In the novel *Moby Dick,* by Herman Melville (1964), Ahab's
    reasonable cause of action is purely commercial: he hunts
    whales for money. But his motive of action is deeply personal:
    he hunts Moby Dick, the white whale, out of revenge because
    Moby Dick took off his leg. The incongruity between Ahab's
    reason and motive of action is evident from the moment he
    brings the conflict into open confrontation by acting on his
    motive while disregarding his reason. Melville points this out
    in Starbuck's words. Starbuck says, "I am game for his crooked
    jaw, and for the jaws of Death too, Captain Ahab, if it fairly
    comes in the way of the business we follow; but I came here
    to hunt whales, not my commander's vengeance" (145).

    Ahab's motive is utterly absurd from Starbuck's rational
    point of view. "Vengeance on a dumb brute!" cried Starbuck,
    "that simply smote thee from blindest instinct! Madness! To
    be enraged with a dumb thing, Captain Ahab, seems blasphe-
    mous" (146). But to understand Ahab's motive, we have to
    transcend the rational plane of reality, as Ahab did. Ahab
    sees Moby Dick not just as a wild beast governed by blind in-
    stincts of nature but as the incarnation of a demonic power
    and supreme reason. So Ahab says, "I see in him outrageous
    strength, with an inscrutable malice sinewing it. That in-
    scrutable thing is chiefly what I hate; and be the white whale
    agent, or be the white whale principal, I will wreak that hate
    upon him. Talk not to me of blasphemy, man; I'd strike the
    sun if it insulted me" (146).

    Why Ahab chases Moby Dick may be justified by what he
    sees in the beast. Ahab anticipates that it may be the devil or
    God showing himself through the beast. The mystery of Moby
    Dick, whether it is a phantom of Ahab's mind or the real
    manifestation of the supreme being, entices Ahab to go after
    it. Ahab's motive is typical for a mythological hero who fights
    the monster who oppresses him. The hero must slay the mon-
    ster in order to regain peace of soul. In this story, the monster

slays the hero. (Interesting twist. It brings the story from the mythological level to the realistic.) This fatal consequence merely shows that Ahab's objective is not real, but it does not diminish the realness of his motive. Ahab proved it by acting on it with all consequences involved. Ahab's inner motive is stronger than his fear of death. His inner truth is so convincing that it blinds his reason, as well as his crew's.

Ahab's inner motive is the insulted honor of a man who believes that God created man in his own image, and that God let men have dominion over the earth and all its creatures. With such a conviction, Ahab's quest would be justified by his belief and his hunt after Moby Dick would be an execution of the rights given by God to dominate all beasts. This Judeo-Christian interpretation of Ahab's inner motive is nothing more than my imposition. Though suitable, I think, it is not the only possibility.

There is no simple answer for Ahab's motive. It comes from a mystical source or madness. Melville, in one of the numerous descriptions of Ahab's motive, writes, "Ah, ye admonitions and warnings! why stay ye not when ye come? But rather are ye predictions than warnings, ye shadows! Yet not so much predictions from without, as verifications of the foregoing things within. For with little external to constrain us, the innermost necessities in our being, these still drive us on" (147).

2. The motive (understood as a personal cause of action) explains not only *why* the character has done something, but also why the character has done it in that *particular way*. For example, Hamlet kills Claudius out of revenge because Claudius murdered Hamlet's father, but Hamlet delays his revenge endlessly because he doubts himself. Hamlet's motive is self-doubt. Hamlet's reasonable cause of action is to revenge his slain father. The incongruity of Hamlet's motive and reasonable cause of action is the source of his inner conflict. Otherwise, he would be in conflict only with Claudius.

87

Inner Motive Versus External Motive

The inner motive is determined by the character's internal needs, drives, and aspirations; the external motive is determined by the demands and opportunities in the character's environment. This division is only operational but not essential. The motive—understood as an actual force moving a person to action—comes from within regardless of whether it is determined by external or internal factors. Therefore, it is hard to imagine a character that is motivated by external factors alone (see the example below). Yet, there are characters that act on their inner motive despite the lack of an external, actual opportunity to fulfill it. However, this is only possible if they substitute actual opportunities with fictional ones, reality with illusion (as visionaries, artists, or mad people do, for example).

> *ASSIGNMENT:* Identify the factors that determine your
> character's motive.

For example, Babbitt, the protagonist of Sinclair Lewis' (1922) novel of the same name, is a total conformist. He yields to the demands of the community and grabs its given opportunities, disregarding his inner needs and aspirations as incompatible with outside forces. He does what his community wants him to do, not what he wants to do. It seems that Babbitt replaces the personal motive with the collective motive. But Babbitt, in his final realization, is not happy about it. In his last words he says, "I've never done a single thing I've wanted to in my whole life! I don't know's I've accomplished anything except just get along" (319). Why has he done it then? His gratification was achieving the position of a powerful persona in his community; but his prize was an emptiness of the soul—a gain not worthy of its losses. The external motivational factors alone are not convincing enough to explain Babbitt's conformity. The decisive factor is different: underneath all that conformity, Babbitt has an inner motive. He has low self-esteem that he does not know how to build up other than by being boosted by the fellows of his community. Babbitt's low self-esteem causes him to disregard his own inner needs and aspirations because they are not significant enough for him to make an investment in them.

Kind of Motive

What kind of motive does your character have?

Is your character's motive conscious or subconscious; rational or irrational; archetypal (universal) or idiosyncratic (exclusively individual)? Is your character's motive inclinational or intentional?

The inclinational motives are psychic and/or nature given, understood as the inherited disposition. The intentional motives are mental fixations (for example, a system of values and principles), either self-conceived or acquired. Aristotle came up with similar categories. He divided motives into two basic categories: the motives of passion (typical for pathetic tragedies) and the motives of ethic (typical for ethical tragedies). This division is as right today as it was in Aristotle's time, but it has been invested with a moral interpretation. Setting up passion opposed to ethic implies that what comes from passion, perhaps, is unethical, in the sense that we have bad inclination but good intention. Since Aristotle's time, many moralists have interpreted Aristotle's statement to mean that human beings are by nature evil and can be cured by imposing a moral code through indoctrination. In contrast, the terms *inclination* and *intention* are ethically neutral, in the sense that we have both good and bad inclinations and good and bad intentions.

Inducing or Acquiring the Character's Motive

> Goethe's Faust aptly says: "Im Anfang war die Tat [In the beginning was the deed]." "Deeds" were never invented, they were done; thoughts, on the other hand, are a relatively late discovery of man. First he was moved to deeds by unconscious factors; it was only a long time afterward that he began to reflect upon the causes that had moved him; and it took him a very long time indeed to arrive at the preposterous idea that he must have moved himself—his mind being unable to identify any other motivating force than his own.
> —*Carl G. Jung,* Man and His Symbols

89

"The inner motive is a mystery," the writer may say. It is a given that whenever the writer is not able to explain or justify the character's conduct by rational causes, he or she blames it on the inner motive. Yet the writer is often not able to explain what that inner motive is—he or she may say that the character is prompted by an inner impulse or led by inner drives he cannot resist. Or the writer may say that the character does it because he cannot help himself, that the character was compelled by inner forces beyond his willful control. That's all right, I guess. As a reader I can buy it, trusting the writer; but as an actor how can I perform it without knowing what the character's inner motive is and from where it comes? How does one figure out the inner motive? First, check whether the writer left any clues in the text. But if there are no clues, discover the inner motive of the character on your own through improvisation. The inner motive of human conduct is a puzzle that in drama we hope to solve.

ASSIGNMENT: Acquire or induce the character's motive.

Approaches

1. Set up the factors that determine your character's motive and condition yourself by them. Simply motivate yourself the way your character did. Keep in mind that the motive is the personal cause of action, so in order to make the conditioning work, make it personal. Set yourself for the quest: "What would I do *if* I had the motive and the cue for passion that the character has?"[1] Would you behave and act as your character does? If yes, your motive is right; if not, either your motive or you are wrong for the part.
2. If you don't know your character's motive in advance because it is either subconcious or the writer failed to reveal it, you are

---

[1] *Refers to the line from* The Tragedy of Hamlet, Prince of Darkness (*Shakespeare 1974*) *"What would he do had he the motive and [the cue] for passion that I have?" 2.2. 560–562*

expected to discover it yourself through improvisation. Simply perform the action first, and then ask yourself, *"Why* have I done it?" You do it because you have an occasion to do it, and by that you want to activate an inner motive that was supposedly dormant in your subconscious until now. You should be able to realize what the inner motive is through experience in your own mind and psyche.

Leitmotiv

The leitmotiv is a reoccurring motive. It motivates the character's behavior and actions throughout the play repeatedly in the same or similar fashion. For example, Othello's leitmotiv is jealousy; Macbeth's is ambition; Shylock's is avarice; Romeo and Juliet's is love.

> *ASSIGNMENT:* Define the leitmotiv of your character. (The chapter on action describes how to work on motives of particular actions.)

Note: It appears that the leitmotiv of the protagonist is the subject or leading theme of the entire play. The other characters' leitmotivs are subjects or themes of the subplots or particular scenes.

Character Choice

I choose myself, not in my
being, but in my manner of
being.

Jean-Paul Sartre,
Being and Nothingness

The actor has no option to make his or her own choice(s) while in the character because all choices are already made by the author of the play. The character in the play is a fictional person who already made all the choices, and as result, his or her destiny is already fulfilled: realized in action, expressed in words and gestures.

Let's settle it once and for all that the actor does not make any unique choices but instead emulates the character's choices. Does this sound uncreative to you? I understand, I had a hard time with this myself. Yet the actor's creativity lies not in creating the character but in bringing it to life. The author gives a blueprint of the character; the actor must discover how it works in his or her own body and mind.

For example, the actor playing Hamlet has no other choice but to kill Polonius (who is hiding behind the arras in Gertrude's closet) in a rush action, mistaking him for King Claudius. The actress playing Hedda Gabler has no other choice but to burn Eilert Lovborg's manuscript in a cruelly calculated act of envy. The actor playing Mr. Humbert has no other choice but to abuse sexually his little protegee, Lolita, with the subtlety of a butterfly collector.

Here is the paradox: whatever the actor does is done not from his personal choice but the character choice, yet it must appear as if it were the actor's own choice. Naturally, there's no problem if it happens that the actor's and the character's choices are exactly the same. In this instance it is enough that the actor asks herself, "What would I do if I were in the same situation as the character is in the play?" And as a result of this simple conditioning, the actor has a natural impulse to do exactly the same as the character does in the play. But if not? What if the actor's personal choice is different than the character's in the same situation? For example, the actor who is playing Hamlet would never personally kill anyone standing behind the arras without first making sure it was the right guy.

Actors often experience a personal resistance to act upon the character's choice in the play because that choice is not in the realm of the actor's personal character. This is expected because most characters the actor portrays are quite different than the actor's personal character. To remedy this, the actor must suspend his own personal character altogether so it does not obstruct his possibilities of acting out characters other than his own. The actor must liberate herself from her personal character in order to be free to make other choices. The actor must put on hold his own personal commitments in order to discover the potential possibility to commit to another choice. In short, the actor has to reject her own character in order to acquire another character on the premise that one can't act in two characters at the same time. Achieving that involves remaking your own psychophysical makeup through instrumental conditioning. However, it is important to stress that this remaking is done on the actor's terms, which means being conditioned not by actuality but by fiction.

Conditioning

What would you do, feel, and think if you were in the situation of the character?

> ASSIGNMENT 1: Put yourself into the situation of the character and experience his circumstances from your own point of view and by your own emotions. Take this quest "What would you do, feel, and think if *you* were in the situation of the character?" literally. So do as you please, express yourself freely, even if it means that you don't behave and act as the character in the play at all. The point of this exercise is to explore yourself in the situation of the character, searching for both your own choices and spontaneity.

Being in the *same situation* and being affected by the *same circumstance* as the character may or may not make you behave and act as the character in the play. One makes choices based not only on the situation and circumstance but also on the individual disposition.

> ASSIGNMENT 2: Define your personal choices and compare them with the character choices.

    my choice   character choice

Is your and the character's choice the same or different?

If your and the character's choices differ from each other, condition yourself further, until you find the motivations to behave and act as your character does in the play. Instead of asking yourself what you would do, feel, and think in the situation of the character, now ask on which condition you would do, feel, and think as the character does in the play.

ASSIGNMENT 3: Define the condition.

If there's no such real condition on which you would behave and act as the character in the play, and you still are not able to overcome your resistance to do it, condition yourself by fiction on the assumption that you have a free will to commit any possible and impossible act in your imagination.

Ask yourself, If I behave and conduct myself as the character, make exactly the same choices, and commit the same acts, what kind of consequences would I have to bear? How would I be affected? How would I change?

Appendix A
The Character Chart

I. Body

How does the character appear?
Define the features and the qualities of the character's body, its appearance, movement, temperament, and center.

APPEARANCE

Visualize the appearance of the character based on the description in the play. Describe his or her looks, build, posture, and carriage of the body.

MOVEMENT

The movement is induced by the actor's impulses that are stirred by emotions and mental attitudes. But it works in reverse, too. The particular kind of movement induces a corresponding emotional state and in consequence influences the mental attitude. There are four general kinds of movements (categorized according to their dynamics): explosive, molding, volatile, and fluid (or floating.) These movements correspond with the four main temperaments: choleric, phlegmatic, sanguine, and melancholic.

a. **What is the kind of movement of your character in general?** Define it and find the correspondence with temperament.

Example: Explosive movement: rapidly erupting, bursting or rupturing, irregularly staccato in rhythm.

b. **Describe the movement found in gestures and walk.**

Example: Abrupt, erratic gestures. Jerky or stormy walk, body makes sudden turns, heels stomp the ground hard.

TEMPERAMENT

The temperament may be defined as an emotional state to which one is inclined to submit most often. Traditional psychology defines temperament in four main categories: choleric, phlegmatic, sanguine, and melancholic. Your character may fit into one of the above categories or be a combination of a few of them.

a. **What is the temperament of your character?** Define it and find the correspondence with the movement.

Example: Choleric temperament: fierce, hyper, and irritable.

CENTER

The center focuses your whole being into one spot, and it serves as the energy source of your activity. The center coordinates the movement of your body, motivating your behavior, actions, and speech.

a. **Establish the location of your character's center.**

Example: If the main disposition of your character is thoughtfulness, you would locate the center in your head.

b. **Stimulate your center by investing it with imaginary qualities.**

Example: For a wise man you would imagine a big, shining, and radiating center in your head. Whereas, for a stupid, fanatic, or narrow-minded type of person you would imagine a small, tense, and hard center in your head.

Note: The center serves you for the character as a whole, but you can use it for different scenes and separate movements. The center can be located within or outside the body; it can be fixed in one place or shift.

Example 2: For a shrewd man with a keenly penetrating mind, you may imagine a sharp, piercing center located a few feet outside your eyes or forehead.

II. **Emotions**

What does the character want?
Define the qualities of the character's will, desires, and feelings. Will tells you what the character decides to do; desires tell you what the character wants or is compelled to do; and feelings tell you how the character is affected by his or her own conduct.

WILL

Will is both the mental and physical disposition of the character. Will makes decisions and gives commands about what to do. Also, will is the power forcing the person to perform an action.

    a.   **What kind of will does your character have?** Describe its qualities.

Example: Is your character's will strong or weak, decisive or hesitant, dominating or submissive, commanding or obeying, good or ill?

    b.   **What does your character decide to do?** Specify the decisions.

DESIRES

Desire is an emotional counterpart of will. Yet desire, unlike will, arises involuntarily, as an emotional urge, craving, or ache of the body, to perform an action and to fulfill one's real wants and wishes. Desire functions as an emotional drive to perform an action.

    a.   **What is the main desire of your character?** Define it.

    b.   **What does your character desire to do?** Specify this for the performance as a whole and for the particular scenes.

FEELINGS

Feelings can be neither directly ordered by will nor guided by reason. Feelings arise on their own as an involuntary response of the body to the situation the person is in at the given moment. Through feelings the body gives signals, either pleasurable or painful, informing the person whether his or her situation is beneficial or harmful.

    a.   **What kind of feelings is your character experiencing during the play?** Specify the character's feelings.

    b.   **To what (or whom) is your character attracted or repulsed (what does he or she like or dislike)?** Define your character's attractions and repulsions. List them: attracted to/ repulsed by.

III. Thought Pattern

How does your character think?
A thought pattern is your character's habitual way of thinking. Its function is to both organize and integrate the mind into personality or ego. In other words, the thought pattern is your character's habitual way of making his or her own mind.

What kind of thought pattern does your character have?
EXAMPLES: imaginative, associative, demagogic, factual, descriptive, poetic, narrative, scheming, psychoanalytic, intuitive, meditative, superficial, versatile, discriminatory, conceptual, abstract, dialectic, scholastic, absurd, interpretative

What does your character think?
Write down your character's thoughts, selecting them from the text. Thoughts are convictions, beliefs, values, reflections, opinions, and views. They are the makeup of your character's mind.

POINT OF VIEW

Point of view is a personal stand one takes, resulting from the way one perceives, understands, and evaluates things or matters. Point of view, in its basic distinction, can be either individualistic or representative. The individual point of view is the result of the character's own experience and is conceived by the character's own mind; the representative point of view is adopted by the character from already-existing philosophy, ideology, religion, tradition, etc.

a. How does your character view matters discussed in the play?
b. What is the main characteristic of your character's point of view?

EXAMPLES

Individualistic	*Representative*
commonsensical	up-to-date
narrow-minded	provincial
logical	cosmopolitan
absurd	fascistic
impressionistic	chauvinistic
rational	feminist
irrational	Puritan
intuitive	Catholic

ATTITUDE

Attitude is the manner of expressing one's views and thoughts. The attitude shows in facial expressions and gestures and has an emotional coloring. Attitude is a psychophysical personification of the point of view.

a. **What kind of attitude does your character have toward other characters in the play?**

EXAMPLES

positive, negative, naïve, sophisticated, rude, polite, arrogant, humble, conceited, modest, bold, timid, courageous, cowardly, cautious, reckless, rebellious, conformist, self-righteous, tolerant, hypocritical, indignant, venerable, scornful, noble, base, decent, deceitful, magnanimous, petty, patronizing, resentful, pretentious, frank, mischievous, proper, flattering, insulting, bitter, sweet, refined, vulgar, cynical, sincere

---

IV.   The External Circumstances

With what does the character interact?
Describe the surroundings with which the character is in contact and by which he or she is affected. Visualize the space, its objects, and persons.

SPACE
a.   **Describe the places in which your character lives and acts.**
b.   **Define the atmospheres and moods of the places.**
c.   **Identify with the atmospheres and moods.** Let yourself be affected.

OBJECTS
a.   **Identify the personal objects of your character.**
b.   **Animate the objects, operate them, and define their functions.**
c.   **Interact with the objects.** Find your relationship with them.

PERSONS
a.   **Identify the persons with whom your character interacts in the play.**
b.   **Animate the persons into various actions in your imagination.**
c.   **Interact with them.**

V. Actions

What does your character do?

Describe the character's actions; define his or her motivations, objectives, and consequences.

ACTION **What does your character do?**

MOTIVATION **Why does he or she do it?**

OBJECTIVE **What is the aim of the action?**

CONSEQUENCES **What is the result of the action?**

VI.   Internal Circumstances

What would you do if[1] you were in the circumstances of the character?

SELF-DEFINITION (in the circumstances of the character)
Put yourself into the situation of the character and experience his or her circumstances from your own point of view and by your own emotions.

Presence
Establish your presence in the circumstances of the character. Presence is the state of "I am" in a given moment of time and the specific location of space. So, you simply can say: I am in the center of things and events, and everything that surrounds me affects me and matters to me personally; the same circumstances that affect the character's behavior and actions now affect mine. Presence enables you to pass to the next stages: interaction and action.

Interaction
Interact with the surroundings from your personal point of view.

1.   Interact with the atmosphere and moods.
2.   Interact with the objects.
3.   Interact with the other characters in the play.

Actions
Interaction without personal aims may not keep you involved for long and may leave you personally impassive, indifferent, and cold. Create the personal aims of your actions: an objective that has the power to attract your wishes and desires.

Choices
Make your choices; establish your point of view, attitudes, emotional reaction, and objectives, etc.

---

[1]*Refers to Stanislavski's "magical if."*

IDENTIFICATION (with the character)

If your choices and the character's choices differ from each other, condition yourself further until you find the motivations to behave and act as your character does in the play.

Differences
Define the differences between your choices and the character's choices:

My Choices / Character Choices

Conditioning
If I conduct myself as the character, make exactly the same choices, and commit the same acts, what kind of consequences would I have to bear? How would I be affected? How would I change?

Pretty soon you will find that you think and feel as the character does.

Appendix B
Movement for the Actor

Plastic Exercises

Expanding and Contracting

1. Expanding and contracting the body in a soft, continuous, and fluid motion   Gradually expand your whole body into a wide, open gesture; your arms and hands are spread wide above, your head and your feet are far apart. At the same time, inhale gradually: first, into the lower parts of the body, then proceed into the upper parts of the body. Remain in the extended position a few seconds. Imagine that you are becoming larger and larger. As you continue to inhale, imagine that you are inhaling the space in front of and above you.

Now contract your body gradually by collapsing in a slow, fluid motion. At the same time, exhale gradually: first, from the upper parts of the body, then proceed to the lower parts. Imagine that you are becoming smaller and smaller, as if you wanted to disappear from space. It looks as if your body were fainting or melting part by part.

Repeat the exercise by dropping and collapsing your body sideways and backward, three times in each direction.

2. Expanding and contracting the body in a sharp, staccato motion   Expand and contract your body part by part in a hard, staccato motion. Expand by tensing your body progressively, beginning in the center that is located in the solar plexus. Imagine that from the center originates the power that forces and pushes the body to expand in space. Remain in the expanded position for a few seconds and let the power radiate out beyond the boundary of your body.

Now contract by shrinking, crumpling, and collapsing your body part by part. Make your movements separate and distinct.

Repeat the exercise three times.

3. Curving and straightening the spine   Stand upright. Bring your feet together. Join them at the heels and leave a space between the balls of the feet. Bend your spine, curving it gradually. Begin the movement from the lower end of your spine and proceed to the upper end. First, curve the pelvis, tilting it backward. At the same time, bend the knees slowly. Then curve the waist, chest, and the nape of the neck in succession, slowly bending them down low. Finally, drop your neck and head. Also, lower your arms, letting them hang down loosely, and rest your hands on the floor.

Now straighten your spine gradually. Begin the movement from the lower end of the spine and proceed to the upper end. First straighten your knees and pelvis. Then build the spine gradually, vertebra by vertebra. Remain in an erect position for a few seconds, straightening and elongating the spine a little bit more. Imagine that something is pulling you up by the hair on the top of the head.

Repeat, curving and straightening the spine three times. Remain in an erect position for the head and neck exercises.

Head and Neck
1.   *Rotations*   Rotate your head while keeping the rest of the body motionless.
   a)   Rotate your head around the horizontal axis that runs through the tip of your nose and the back of your head. It is a short, small, and light rotary movement up and down. Make sure that your head is relaxed and softly settled on the erect neck.
   b)   Now rotate your head around the vertical axis in a quick and light rotary movement from side to side. Speed up the rotation and then let your head stop by the force of its own inertia.
   c)   Rotate your head around the horizontal axis that runs between your ears. It is a small and light movement, similar to the first rotation.

2. *Rolling the head around the neck*   Keep your neck erect, drop your head loosely down, and roll around the neck.

3. *Neck stretching*
   a) Extend and shrink the neck up and down alternately in a soft, serpentine motion from side to side. It looks like a snake's dance: the neck elongates to its maximum extension and then shrinks, vanishing between the shoulders.
   b) Repeat as before, but make the serpentine motion forward and backward.
   c) Stretch your neck upward as if someone were pulling you up by the ear. Repeat on both sides. Stretch your neck when pulling it up and relax when withdrawing to the initial position. Now stretch your neck upward as if someone were pulling you up by your collar.
   d) Repeat a few times to the side and back. Magnify your movement and involve the whole body. It looks like a string puppet pulled up and dropped down by invisible strings.

4. *Shifting*
   a) Shift your head by pushing it back and forth in a soft, oscillating motion. Now shift your head from side to side.
   b) Shift the head in all four directions in succession and withdraw to the initial position each time. Press when you are pushing out and relax when you are withdrawing.
   c) Rotate the head around the circle on the horizontal plane, stopping at each quarter of the circle. Then rotate your head in full circles continuously, diminishing the size of the circle gradually to zero volume. Next rotate your head in the opposite direction, gradually magnifying the size of the circle at the same time.
   d) Drop your neck and head on the chest loosely and roll them around the trunk. When dropping your neck and head, do it gradually: first, push your head forward; then lower your neck, laying it on the chest; then finally, drop your head down. Next roll the neck and head around the trunk.

Shoulder
1. *Relaxation*   Relax your shoulders by flinging them back and forth in a quick, bouncing motion.
2. *Shifting*
   a)   Shift your shoulders, one at a time, to the four sides in succession: up, forward, down, and back.
   b)   Rotate both your shoulders in circles in opposite directions.
   c)   Extend your arms sideways on a horizontal level and shift your shoulders one at a time to the four directions: up, toward the body, down, then away from the body.
   d)   Rotate your shoulders in a circle, keeping your arms extended as before.
3. *Pulling out and contracting in*   Pull your shoulders out, away from the body, and in, toward the body, alternately. Do this exercise while raising your arms up and then lowering them down gradually, forming half circles on your sides.

   Tense and strain the arm when you pull in and relax when you pull out. Now do it in the opposite way: tense and strain your arm when you pull the shoulder out, and relax, slackening your arm when you pull in.
4. *Flying movement*
   a)   Stretch one arm sideways. Throw your shoulder up and down. The impulse of the movement comes from the shoulder and affects the arm, forearm, and hand in succession. It resembles a wing in motion.
   b)   Repeat the exercise with the other shoulder.
   c)   Repeat the exercise with both shoulders at the same time.
   d)   Repeat the exercise, this time involving the whole body.

Elbows
1. *The forearm rotations*   Stretch your arms sideways. Drop your forearms down, letting them swing loosely in a pendulum-like motion. Then rotate the forearms in circles on the vertical plane. It resembles the movement of propeller blades.
2. *Bending*

a) Stretch your arms and hands sideways on the horizontal level. Bend one elbow upward. Your shoulder and hand remain fixed at the same level. Now straighten your elbow, returning to the initial position. Practice on both elbows alternately.

b) Bend your elbows downward.

3. *Elbow rotation*   Bend both of your elbows and rotate them around the horizontal axis, keeping your shoulders and hands fixed on the horizontal level.

Wrists

1. *Vibrations*   Stretch your arms and hands sideways on the horizontal level. Then drop your forearms down, letting them swing in a light, pendulum-like motion. Induce vibrations in your wrists by shaking them back and forth with quick, short movements. Intensify the vibration and let the other parts of the body be affected. Change the positions of your wrists: raise them gradually upward, in front of your upper body, the palms facing the body. Then turn your palms facing forward and drop your hands, lowering them slowly down.

Incorporate images: imagine that you are shaking the water off your hands then off both hands and arms. Incorporate another image: imagine that a current of electricity flows through your arms and hands; as a result, you should experience the sensation of pins and needles in your fingertips. Now focus the vibrations on one wrist. Then turn your palm upward and incorporate another image: imagine that you have quicksilver in your hand. Let your whole body be affected by the vibrations.

Repeat the exercise once again, ending with the other hand.

2. *Shifting*

a) Place your wrists vertically at shoulder level and shift them from side to side in a soft, oscillating motion. At the same time, keep your elbows and fingertips fixed in a still position. Now shift your wrists back and forth.

b) Shift your wrists, bending them to the four sides and withdrawing to the initial position each time. Push firmly out when bending and relax when withdrawing the wrists.

3. *Rotations* Rotate your wrists around in a circle, stopping after each quarter of a circle. Now rotate your wrists in full circles continuously.

4. *Geometrical movements: straight and curved lines*

a) Poster: Spread an imaginary poster on a wall. Lead your flat hands on the four sides of the poster, spreading it. The effort of movement comes from the wrists: first, lead with your wrists; the hands and arms follow. Involve the whole body, forming it in counterpoint to the movement of your wrists. Identify with the poster: your poster is spread and open; your body is spread and open, too.

b) Cube: Form a large imaginary cube. Lead your flat hands along the cube's surfaces, showing its shape. The effort of movement comes from the wrists. The whole body is involved, moving in counterpoint to the movement of your wrist. Now diminish the size of the cube. Take the diminished cube to one hand and show its weight. Shift the cube from one hand to the other. Now magnify the cube.

c) Ball: Form a large imaginary ball. The movement of your hands shows the curving shape of the ball. The wrists lead the movement. The whole body is involved. Now diminish the size of the ball. Shift the ball from one hand to the other. Keep the ball on one hand while the other moves along the ball's surface. Magnify the ball.

Hands

1. *Relaxation*

a) Relax your hands by shaking and rotating them quickly and lightly.

b) Wriggling movement: Squirm and wriggle your fingers like swarming worms. Involve your palms in the movement and soften the whole hands.

2. *Attaching the hands to the imaginary surface*

110

a) Relax and suspend your hands above the imaginary surface. Then attach your hands to the surface, one after another. Keep your hands flat and extended by pressing the palms against the surface and spreading the fingers apart. Now detach your hands from the surface and withdraw to the initial position by relaxing them, one after another. Repeat the exercise several times. Tense your hands when you attach them and relax when you detach them from the surface. Change the location of the imaginary surface.

b) Repeat the exercise in a quick, bouncy rhythm. Strike your hands on and spring them back from the surface. The movement of your hands is similar to a bouncing ball. It prepares you for the next exercise.

c) Bouncing the ball: Imagine that you have a small ball in your hand. Throw the imaginary ball against the floor and catch it when it bounces back. The movements of your hands identify with the movement of a bouncing ball. Play in various combinations: throwing with one hand and catching with the other, throwing against the front wall, throwing upward, and tossing from hand to hand.

Chest

1. *Shifting*

   a) Place your hands on your hips and shift your chest back and forth in a soft, oscillating motion.

   b) Now shift your chest from side to side in a soft, oscillating motion.

2. *Bending*

   a) First, shift your chest forward, pushing it out; afterward, bend your upper body forward; finally, drop your arms and hands, then your head down, letting them hang loosely. Return to the initial position in one motion. Repeat the exercise sideways and backward, three times in each direction.

   b) Rotation: Bend forward as before, remain in a bent posture, and rotate your upper body around the lower body.

3. *Shifting and rotations*
    a) Place your hands on your hips and shift your chest in four directions, withdrawing each time to the initial position. Press strongly when pushing out; relax when withdrawing.
    b) Rotate your chest around the circle, stopping after each quarter of the circle.
    c) Now rotate your chest in full circles continuously. Make your rotations rhythmical by accenting the forward position. Next, rotate your chest in the opposite direction with the accent on the backward position.
4. *Stretch your arms and hands sideways and keep them in a fixed position through the following exercises*
    a) Shift your chest in four directions, withdrawing each time to the initial position.
    b) Rotate your chest around the circle, stopping after each quarter of the circle.
    c) Now rotate your chest in full circles continuously. Make your rotations rhythmical by placing the accent forward.
    d) Rotate your chest in the opposite direction and place the accent backward.
5. *Shift the upper parts of the body in succession as follows:*
    a) Push your chest out, then your shoulders, and finally your head. Repeat the exercise in four directions.
    b) Shift the upper body, from the waist up in one block. Do this in all four directions. Withdraw into the initial position each time. It looks as if your body were cut in half at the waist and the torso became shifted.
    c) Move in space while shifting the upper and lower parts of the body against each other in counterpoint.

Loins
1. *Turns and rotations*
    a) Turn the hips, swaying them back and forth in a soft, oscillating motion. Now turn the hips, swaying them from side to side.

b) Turn the hips in four directions with a twist up at the same time.

c) Rotate the hips in circles, accenting the forward thrust. Now reverse the direction with the accent on the backward thrust.

2. *Large turns and rotations*

a) Push your hips, swaying them backward and forward while standing alternately on your toes and heels.

b) Push your hips, swaying them from side to side while standing alternately on your toes and heels. Involve your hands, pushing them sideways in the opposite direction to the movement of your hips, as if you were pushing against the side of a wall.

c) Stretch your hands sideways and rotate your hips around a large circle.

d) Shift your hips around a cube and a cube around the hips at the same time, pushing against each other in a circle.

3. *Shifting by pushing against the object* Shift your hips in four directions while pushing against an imaginary object. Withdraw to the initial position each time.

Push the imaginary object forward. Imagine an object close to your loins. Place your flattened hands on the side of the object closest to your body. Place them at hip level, directing the fingertips downward. Push the object forward. Your hands move in the direction of the object and your loins withdraw in the opposite direction at the same time and distance.

Now push the imaginary object sideways. In the initial position, the object and left hip are close to each other. Place your left hand on the object's side surface at hip level. Push the object to the right and the hips in opposite direction at the same time and distance. Repeat the movement on the opposite side.

Push the imaginary object backward. The object and your hips are close to each other. Place both your hands on the object's side surface at hip level. Push the object backward and your hips forward, shifting them in opposite directions at the same time and distance.

4. *Pushing away the body*   Push an imaginary object away from the body in various positions.

5. *Pulling the rope*   Pull the rope toward your body. In the initial position your hands reach for the rope away from your body, and at the same time, your body, mostly the loins, withdraws in the opposite direction.

   While drawing the rope, your hands move toward your body, and your body, mostly the loins, moves toward the hands, contrary to the movement of the rope.

Feet

1. *Pushing insteps out*

   a)   Bring your feet together and parallel. Push your insteps out, alternately pressing your toes firmly into the ground.

   b)   Now shift your feet from heels to toes and from toes to heels alternately. One foot stands on its toes while the other is on its heel. Push your insteps out and raise the toes above the ground as far as they can go. Your whole body is involved in the motion, as if you were walking in one place. Your elbows move back and forth contrary to your knees; your hips are swaying, moving backward and returning loosely to the vertical position. Tense your body while moving the hips back and relax while returning.

   c)   Now add another movement element to your exercise: pivot one foot to the side, turning it on the heel as if it were a hinge. Your other foot stands on the toes at the same time, as before. Then return to the initial position, bringing your feet in parallel, and repeat the same motion, pivoting the other foot. The movement of your whole body changes a little bit, too. The balance is shifted forward by placing the weight of your whole body on your toes as well as pushing your hips forward. Tense your body

while pushing your hips forward and relax while withdrawing them.

2. *Mime walks*

    a) Now proceed to the mime walk: prolong the pivoting of
       the foot, thrusting it backward, keeping the sole of the
       foot low to the ground. Establish a walking rhythm with
       an accent on the forward thrust of the body.

    b) Walk thrusting the feet forward alternately.

    c) Walk thrusting the feet sideways.

    d) Walk thrusting the feet backward again in a quicker tempo.

    e) Speed up the tempo and run.

    f) Walk thrusting the feet forward and backward in a slow
       tempo.

    g) Skate.

    h) Jump.

Knees

1. *Knee vibrations*

    a) Induce vibrations in your knees. The exercise proceeds in
       three stages, as follows.

       1. Walk across a room from heels to toes alternately.
          Push the insteps out and raise the toes above the
          ground as far as they can go.

       2. Walk flat-footed in short and quick steps. Sustain
          the movement from heels to toes, though it becomes
          a hardly visible motion of the soles, lightly rolling on
          the floor.

       3. Induce vibrations in your knees by moving them
          back and forth quickly in an oscillating motion. Let
          the whole body be affected by the vibrations. Speed
          up the vibrations but don't tense the body. Remain
          light and loose. As a result, your body becomes both
          invigorated and relaxed.

    b) Practice the vibrations while imagining that you are on a
       moving train.

Balance and Orientation in Space

The directions in the following exercise refer to the four walls of the space.

Stand on your toes, extending your body up. Squat down slowly, raising your hands upward at the same time. Then stand up slowly, lowering your hands at the same time. While in the standing position, elongate your body, imagining that someone is pulling you up by your hair.

Then sit down (as if on a chair), and extend your hands and right leg downstage, as if reaching into the far distance. Make a prolonged step forward, standing on your right foot and raising the left leg behind you. Your body extends horizontally; your face reaches forward and your left foot backward. The arms are close to the body and reaching backward.

Now make a quarter turn, extending your body sideways on a vertical plane. Your body is spreading in four directions: your head and left foot sideways (in opposition), and your left arm and hand stretch upward while the right arm and hand stretch downward, also in opposition.

Next continue with another quarter turn and close your body as if you were closing something inside yourself. Then open your body, straightening your spine vertically and opening your leg and arms to the side. The left leg extends downstage, and one hand extends downstage while the other extends upstage.

Now make the next quarter of a turn. Extend both your hands upstage and your left leg downstage horizontally. Then make one step downstage. Your feet are far apart on the ground; the knees are bent; the hands are stretched horizontally, one downstage and the other upstage.

Then make a half turn, facing downstage. Stand up and bring your feet together in the initial position.

Repeat the whole combination on the other leg.

References

Aristotle. 1961. *Aristotle's Poetics*. Trans. S. H. Butcher. New York: Hill and Wang.

Beckett, Samuel. 1954. *Waiting for Godot*. New York: Grove Press.

Campbell, Joseph. 1988. *The Power of Myth with Bill Moyers*. Edited by B. Sue Flowers. New York: Doubleday.

Cassirer, Ernst. 1971. *Esej o Czlowieku* Original title: *An Essay on Man: An Introduction to a Philosophy of Human Culture*. Warsaw, Poland: Czytelnik.

Chekhov, Michael. 1953. *To the Actor: On the Technique of Acting*. New York: Harper & Row.

Craig, E. Gordon. 1966. "The Art of the Theatre." In *Wroclawski Teatr Pantomimy*, edited by Janina Hera. Wroclaw, Poland: Prasa.

Dostoyevsky, Fyodor. 1961. *Notes from Underground*. Trans. Andrew R. MacAndrew. New York: A Signet Classic.

Durant, Will. 1926. *The Story of Philosophy*. New York: Simon and Schuster.

Fitz Gerald, Gregory. 1971. *Modern Satiric Stories*. Glenview, IL: Scott, Foresman.

Grebanier, Bernard. 1961. *Playwriting*. New York: Harper & Row.

Hagen, Uta. 1973. *Respect for Acting*. New York: Macmillan.

Howard, David, and Edward Mabley. 1993. *The Tools of Screenwriting: A Writer's Guide to the Craft and Elements of a Screenplay*. New York: St. Martin's Press.

Jung, Carl G. 1964. *Man and His Symbols*. New York: Dell.

Laban, Rudolf. 1950. *The Mastery of Movement*. Ed. Lisa Ullmann. Estover, Plymouth: Macdonald & Evans; Fromme and London: Butler & Tanner Ltd.

Lewis, Sinclair. 1922. *Babbitt*. New York: Harcourt, Brace & World.

Melville, Herman. 1964. *Moby Dick*. New York: Airmont.

Musil, Robert. 1971. *The Man Without Qualities* Original title: *Der Mann Ohne Eigenschaften*. Warsaw, Poland: Panstwowy Instytut Wydawniczy.

Nabakov, Vladimir. 1977. *Lolita*. New York: Berkley Books.

Sartre, Jean-Paul. 1956. *Being and Nothingness: An Essay on Phenomenological Ontology*. Trans. and with introduction by Hazel E. Barnes. New York: Philosophical Library.

Shakespeare, William. 1974. *The Tragedy of Hamlet, Prince of Denmark*. In *The Riverside Shakespeare*. Boston: Houghton Mifflin.

————. 1974. *The Tragedy of Macbeth*. In *The Riverside Shakespeare*. Boston: Houghton Mifflin.

Stanislavski, Constantin. 1961. *Creating a Role*. Trans. Elizabeth Reynolds Hapgood, ed. Hermine I. Popper. New York: Routledge, Chapman and Hall.

Strasberg, Lee. 1987. *A Dream of Passion*. Edited by Evangeline Morphos. Boston and Toronto: Little, Brown.

Tomaszewski, Henryk. 1979. Mime Workshops at Wroclawski Teatr Pantomimy. Wroclaw, Poland.

Williams, Tennessee. 1953. *A Streetcar Named Desire*. New York: Dramatists Play Service.